# Reflective Practice in ESL Teacher Development Groups

# Reflective Practice in ESL Teacher Development Groups

## From Practices to Principles

Thomas S.C. Farrell
*Brock University, Canada*

First published 2013 by
PALGRAVE MACMILLAN

Palgrave Macmillan in the UK is an imprint of Macmillan Publishers Limited, registered in England, company number 785998, of Houndmills, Basingstoke, Hampshire RG21 6XS.

Palgrave Macmillan in the US is a division of St Martin's Press LLC, 175 Fifth Avenue, New York, NY 10010.

Palgrave Macmillan is the global academic imprint of the above companies and has companies and representatives throughout the world.

Palgrave® and Macmillan® are registered trademarks in the United States, the United Kingdom, Europe and other countries

ISBN: 978–0–230–29255–0

This book is printed on paper suitable for recycling and made from fully managed and sustained forest sources. Logging, pulping and manufacturing processes are expected to conform to the environmental regulations of the country of origin.

A catalogue record for this book is available from the British Library.

A catalog record for this book is available from the Library of Congress.

# Contents

# List of Tables

# Acknowledgements

I would like to thank the three ESL teachers who allowed me to enter their professional lives for a while so that we all could learn from their experiences. After reflecting with these wonderful teachers I realize even more than ever how complex teaching is and how professional the three teachers really are. I would also like to thank the SSHRC of Canada.

# Introduction: From Practices to Principles

## Introduction

Research on teaching and teachers in the field of general education has refocused somewhat over the recent past to what teachers actually do. In other words, research has started to examine the different ways in which experienced teachers understand their practice in relation to their accumulated career experiences by listening to their voices and getting their views (Hargraves, 1996). This research *with* rather than *on teachers* now includes the teachers' understandings of their profession with the idea that teachers can be generators of research rather than always being consumers of research by others (see also research approach later in this chapter). In English language teaching, Freeman (1996) has pointed out the importance of listening to teachers' voices about what they do because he says that it is necessary to put teachers at the centre of telling their stories. Freeman (1996: 89) maintains that putting teachers in front and centre in terms of listening to what they do actually follows the jazz maxim: "You have to know the story in order to tell the story". That said, not much has really happened in the English Language Teaching (ELT) field as we have not heard many of the voices of experienced English as a Second Language (ESL) teachers and their various experiences over their years of teaching ESL.

So, one of the main purposes of this book is really to give this voice to experienced ESL teachers and add to the corpus of what experienced ESL teachers understand about their own practices rather than what researchers think they should understand. *Reflective Practice in ESL Teacher Development Groups: From Practices To Principles* helps provide such a voice by exploring the professional journeys and experiences of three experienced ESL teachers in Canada as relayed (through discussions,

1

interviews, and journal writing and classroom observations) in their self-initiated teacher reflection group as part of their professional development. I (as author and group facilitator) have been given their permission to tell their story. By documenting their journey and experiences I hope readers will be able to look into their worlds from their point of view. According to Bullough (1997: 19) telling such a story "[i]s a way of getting a handle on what [they] believe, on models, metaphors and images that underpin action and enable meaning making, on [their] theories".

In telling their story by relaying what they discussed, wrote, and reflected on during classroom observations you will see principles emerge from practice. As Bullough (1997: 19) suggested, "Through storytelling, personal beliefs become explicit, and in being made explicit they can be changed, where change is warranted, and a new or different story results; we behold differently". *Reflective Practice in ESL Teacher Development Groups: From Practices To Principles* thus gives voice to experienced ESL teachers that may otherwise go unheard and it also outlines and discusses how their personal tacitly held beliefs were made explicit in group meetings and journal writing and how they began to theorize from this new knowledge of what they do in their classrooms. Indeed, for experienced teachers theory is not important if it is not directly linked to practice and Bullough (1997: 20) has even gone so far as to say: "unless theories come from practice, they will not apply to practice". I also agree with Williams and Burden (1997: 2) when they say that "Each individual constructs his or her own reality". Within this reality I believe all teachers have a personal framework of how languages should be taught and learned. In other words, I believe all teachers construct their own representations of teaching. My role as reflective facilitator throughout the reflective project reported on in *Reflective Practice in ESL Teacher Development Groups: From Practices To Principles* was to help the teachers make these usually tacitly held prior beliefs explicit. I shall address my role in more detail later in this chapter.

## From practices to principles

*Reflective Practice in ESL Teacher Development Groups: From Practices To Principles* is a book about teachers and for teachers, and teacher educators and administrators. I shall begin by explaining the subtitle *(From Practices To Principles)* first because it highlights the uniqueness of the book. This subtitle emerged from my readings of Bullough's (1997: 13) work in which he noted that "[p]rinciples emerge from practice; we practice our principles, and in practicing and confronting our limitations often we discover just what those principles are". There are several parts to this wonderful quote that are very instructive and insightful for teachers. After many years of teaching, teachers tend to forget their principles but this does not mean they do not have them. What he is also saying is that we should reflect on our practice and by reflecting on our practices we can discover just what our limitations are and then confront them and ultimately learn how to overcome them. As Bullough (1997: 13) notes, "to teach is to testify; to bear witness of a way of being in and understanding the world and we can 'bear witness' by reflecting on our practices and make the tacit about our practices more explicit to ourselves and others" As you will read later in this book some our limitations can centre on the concept of "plateauing" in teaching but we may not be able to notice we have plateaued unless we consciously reflect on where we are at in our teaching careers. Chapter 4 will relay how the three experienced teachers reflected on their careers through group discussions and how these reflective talks lead to the realization of the very real possibility of plateauing for them all.

Yes, *From Practices to Principles* may sound like a strange way to order the development of principles or theory. Usually teachers are educated and encouraged to access their theory or principles first and then look at how these can be transformed into practice; or to work from theory to practice. I agree that this is a good way for novice teachers to approach their teaching. However, what happens when teachers have spent many years in the classroom and have only focused on refining their practices rather than articulating their principles? Indeed Dewey (1916: 169) has noted: "An ounce of experience is better than a ton of theory simply because it is only in experience that any theory has vital and veritable significance". I would add that these experiences do not mean much unless we consciously reflect on them so that we can decide how they have shaped us as teachers.

*Reflective Practice in ESL Teacher Development Groups: From Practices To Principles* has a unique approach to continuing teacher development in that it takes a "practices to principles" approach by attempting to access the accumulated experiences of three experienced ESL teachers in Canada as they reflected on their practices over a two-year period in a self-initiated teacher reflection group. It highlights their collaborative development rather than their individual development and the value of their "local" understanding of their practices. Of course, I realize that these "local" understandings may have limitations in terms of their generalizability because of the relatively small number of teachers (three) studied and their specific context. As a qualitative researcher I would like to point out that I usually do not focus on the generalizability of research findings because I am trying only to convey "local" understandings and interpretations with "thick" descriptions of what is. Indeed, Creswell (1994: 159) has pointed out that the purpose of a qualitative research is "not to generalize findings, but to form a unique interpretation of events". Lincoln and Guba (1985: 316) have also argued that a qualitative researcher "cannot specify the external validity of an enquiry; he or she can provide only thick description necessary to enable someone interested in making a transfer to reach a conclusion about whether transfer can be contemplated as a possibility". I have attempted to provide such a thick description with the details presented in each chapter of this book.

Throughout *Reflective Practice in ESL Teacher Development Groups: From Practices To Principles* I also have attempted to live up to my responsibility to provide a large enough database with specific examples of the teachers' direct quotes and writings "that makes transferability judgments possible on the part of potential appliers" (Lincoln and Guba, 1985: 316). So researchers and teacher educators can make their own judgments regarding my interpretations. Indeed, teacher educators can replicate this work so that they can compare their findings to those reported on in this book and add to the corpus of what experienced ESL teachers really do when they reflect on their practices.

How reliable are the results reported on in this book? The reliability of any qualitative research really depends on whether the findings would be repeated if the study were replicated in similar conditions (with similar subjects and context). Like the problem of external validity, the specificity of a qualitative study makes it difficult to replicate. Following Creswell (1994: 159), I have stated "the researcher's position, the central assumptions, the selection of informants, and the biases and values of the researcher" in order to increase the chances of replicating the study in another setting. Hence future studies can address this issue by using a comparative approach to demonstrate the similarities and differences across a number of settings. That said, I believe that much of what is described and discussed in this book may have relevance for an individual language teacher's practice and context as well as teacher educators and administrators. Thus, by writing this book I have attempted to, as Meister and Ahrens (2011: 1) have noted, "to enter the conceptual world of the participants to understand it as they do and to portray that understanding so that it will be insightful and illuminating for others". Teacher educators can also enter these experienced teachers' worlds by reflecting on the details presented in each chapter. Teacher educators may find it interesting to note that the final chapter on teacher expertise concludes that teacher expertise is not the direct result of teacher experience; rather it involves teachers taking a critically reflective approach to their work such as what the three teachers in this book did. This conclusion has implications for teacher education programes that tend to focus on delivering methods type courses rather than preparing teachers for the realities of what they will face in real classrooms. It also has implications for teacher education programes who may want to prepare their teachers for lifelong careers in that the actions necessary for reaching the status of teacher as expert involve knowledge of reflective practice and all that entails. Teacher educators can gain such knowledge from reading the contents of this book.

*Reflective Practice in ESL Teacher Development Groups: From Practices To Principles* is also for administrators. Many books for teachers tend to forget those that work closest with teachers: their administrators. Some administrators are excellent while others are not so helpful for teachers and this maybe because they are under pressure from ministries or owners to look at the bottom line of finances rather than the individuals who work from them. This book can help administrators see what experienced teachers actually do and what issues are important for them because these issues can also be very important for the institution/school. For example, take the issue of teacher plateauing (see Chapters 2 and 9 for more on plateauing), which has enormous implications for institutions because teachers who are not really performing in the classroom will negatively impact students who in turn may not want to register from more courses and this would have negative consequences for the institution/school's bottom line – the same bottom line many administrators tend to spend all their time watching.

So administrators can use *Reflective Practice in ESL Teacher Development Groups: From Practices To Principles* to reflect on the various issues impacting their teachers and, more specifically, can try to find ways to help teachers cope with teacher plateauing. They can begin their reflections on becoming familiar with teacher life cycles and placing their teachers on particular points while realizing they may have needs at these various points in their careers. Indeed, if they have more of an understanding of teacher career cycles and a teacher's movement in and out of these cycles, they can help prevent career stagnation for certain staff members and thus keep the students happy too. Indeed, if institutions want to encourage their ESL teachers to perform better, they should find ways to support their teachers and boost their morale by recognizing and affirming (verbally or otherwise) their important role within that institution. This support can come from the administration by providing regular time for teachers to meet together so that they collaborate and build supportive bonds with other teachers and the administration as they enter their mid-career years. For example, institutions could encourage the creation of teacher reflection groups similar to the one reported on in this book to help break feelings of isolation and overcome feelings of plateauing.

*Reflective Practice in ESL Teacher Development Groups: From Practices To Principles* is about the intense critical reflections of three experienced ESL college teachers in their mid-careers. Specifically, it outlines and discusses their mid-career reflections over a two-year period through the use of regular group discussions, regular writing in a teacher journal, and interviews before, during, and after the period of reflection. The three participants (for reasons of anonymity called T1 (teacher 1), T2 (teacher 2), T3 (teacher 3)) in the teacher reflection group were all experienced female ESL college teachers in Canada. Each teacher had an initial qualification in teaching ESL (a BA in Applied Linguistics) and a further qualification at the certificate at a more advanced level (Certificate in Teaching English as a Second Language (TESL)). In addition, T1 had an MA degree in Applied Linguistics with a major in TESL. Each teacher had at least 15 years of experience teaching English as a second language. Thus the book is about real practicing teachers' experiences and reflections and looks at teacher development through the prism of their eyes, thoughts, behaviors, and writings.

The genesis of the teacher group is unique in that this researcher was approached by the three participants and asked if he would be willing to facilitate their professional development as facilitator of the group through the use of reflective practice. This makes such a group unique as it is a self-initiated teacher reflection group, and so I asked the teachers why they wanted to engage in such group reflections. All three teachers said that they felt the need to examine their practice; specifically, T1 responded that she was feeling some burnout and in need of a new challenge with her teaching; T2 mentioned that she felt that she needed to look at her practice; T3 said she felt that after many years as an ESL teacher, she need some "time-out to look at my teaching". T2 said that she became an ESL teacher "because I had an undergraduate degree in Linguistics" but that at first she only "chose TESL as a temporary career". T2 continued: "I thought TESL would allow me to travel and to pay off my student loans and then go back to school and start a 'real' career". However, she never did start that "real career" and now as she realizes this is in fact her "real career"; T2 continued: "Well, here I am many years later, in my real career but very happy that I did not change my career path".

All three teachers asked me (author) to act as a facilitator for the group as they were familiar with the type of work I do. My role was to enter the professional worlds of three ESL college teachers as they reflected on their work in this self-initiated teacher reflection group and then to present these reflections to the wider community – with their permission I recorded, transcribed, and interpreted the discussions, interviews, and teacher journals with their permission – as one attempt to unwrap "the shroud of silence in which our practice is wrapped" (Brookfield, 1995: 136). Throughout the reflection process I attempted to keep anxiety levels as low as possible by building an atmosphere of openness and trust. There were no boundaries set about the topics for each group discussion and the teachers decided themselves what they wanted to talk about at each of the 13 group meetings. I shared my perceptions openly with the group as a participant-observer in the group discussions where appropriate (Clair, 1998; Jorgensen, 1989); however, I did not reflect as much on my own teaching. Rather, I attempted to manage the process so that the teacher-participants could feel they had space in which to reflect on their own practice.

## Bottom-up professional development

Professional development for ESL teachers has more often than not consisted of district or administration-mandated courses and one-stop workshops conducted by outside "experts" in a top-down approach to the dissemination of knowledge in which teachers are subsequently expected to translate into action in order to improve their practice. While suggestions for improving practice with such a top-down delivered system may be well intentioned, its real impact is limited because teachers may find that many of the ideas presented are often conceptually and practically far removed from the reality of their particular classrooms. In fact, throughout their careers, many language teachers have been expected to learn about their own profession not by studying their own experiences, but by studying the findings of outside so-called experts. Johnson and Golombek (2002: 3), however, called for a new approach within TESOL that recognizes teachers as "legitimate knowers, producers of legitimate knowledge, and as capable of constructing and sustaining their own professional practice over time". In such an emerging emancipatory paradigm of professional development, language teachers take on the role of reflective practitioners where they actively assume a critical stance towards their work (Cormany, Maynor, and Kalnin, 2005). The implications of such an approach to language teacher's professional development underscores the need for a shift from having teachers develop in isolation to where they are supported in a group while reflecting on their work. This was the basis for the formation of the teacher-initiated reflection group and its facilitator reported on in this book.

The reflective process for the teacher reflection involved regular group discussions, journal writing, some classroom observations, and pre- and post-interviews of each teacher. This bottom-up approach to professional development can significantly enhance knowledge on what counts for professional development of ESL teachers and can promote ESL teacher-initiated professional development that is more focused towards classroom realities, based on knowledge that is co-constructed through engagement with experience, and systematic reflections, and is grounded in real teaching situations. In addition, the suggestions presented in this book can be operationalized as possible benchmarks and standards for future ESL or English as a Foreign Language (EFL) teacher reflection groups and development programmes worldwide.

## Research approach

I will now briefly point out the theoretical framework I used to oversee the research conducted with the teachers. Kiely and Davis (2010: 278) have noted that the continued professional development (CPD) of ESL teachers has moved from a "transmission" approach (or deficit approach) where deficits in teacher knowledge are addressed by appropriate input from theory and research conducted by experts, to a "transformation" approach where the "goal is to support teachers in understanding and enhancing their [own] practice". As Kiely and Davis (2010: 278) have observed, "[t]ransformational CPD is practice based, with learning grounded in teachers" own classrooms'. It is the transformational approach to CPD that is relevant to the study reported on in this book in that it involved teachers in a teacher reflection group analysing and reflecting on their own work both inside and outside the classroom. In other words, within this approach the teacher moves from a consumer of others' research to a generator of research – "in short, a reflective practitioner who theories practice" (Wright, 2010: 267).

### Data collection

Qualitative research procedures were used in the collection and analysis of the data in the study outlined in this book (Bogdan and Bilken, 1982; Glesne and Peshkin, 1992). Data were collected over a two-year period with weekly group meetings during the academic terms of the first year and follow-up meetings during the second year. All three teachers agreed to commit themselves as much as possible to attend all the group meetings, and attend interviews before, during, and after the reflective period. There were 13 two-hour (average) group meetings in total. There were also follow-up interviews (all recorded and transcribed) throughout the first and second years and at the end of the reflective process in order to clarify previous insights gained. All group discussions and interviews were audio-recorded and transcribed. In addition, throughout the period of reflection the teachers agreed to write regularly in a teacher journal. Initially, all three teachers agreed that each participant would keep an ongoing journal account of their experiences during the period of the group's existence. They agreed at the beginning that they could write about anything, whenever they wanted, but they also agreed to write at least one entry after an "event" was experienced; an "event" was to include a class observation and/or discussion, and a group meeting.

## Data analysis

Because of the sheer volume of data, analysis was ongoing and recursive all during the period of data collection (Glesne and Peshkin, 1992; Lincoln and Guba, 1985; Merriam, 2001). As Merriam (2001: 162) has noted, "data that have been analyzed while being collected are both parsimonious and illuminating". For coding of the data, the theoretical framework that was employed in the study was grounded in the existing literature on teacher reflection and followed a two-pronged approach: the first was the use of codes intended to explore issues identified in the literature. However, because of the "grounded approach" that the study observed, I also looked for interesting possibilities from the data and invented codes for further exploration. The teacher reflection group reported on in this book used group discussions and teaching journals as their main tools for reflection. Then transcripts from these reflective modes (group discussions and journal writing) were scanned again for a closer examination of the three *teaching beliefs*, and *teacher roles*, as well as important *critical incidents* that occurred in their teaching during the period of systematic reflections. Specifically, a total of 25,200 lines of text (from group discussions, interviews and journal entries) were scanned, coded, recoded, and analysed for references to these issues. Then at the end of the data collection period all data were scanned once more for accurate interpretation of patterns and themes (Bogdan and Biklen, 1982; Lincoln and Guba, 1985).

In order to establish the trustworthiness (a qualitative measurement similar to reliability and validity) of the findings, I (along with a research assistant) assessed the quality of the data by checking for its "credibility"

(Lincoln and Guba, 1985: 300). Lincoln and Guba (1985: 301) suggest that "credible findings will be produced" by "the investment of sufficient time to achieve certain purposes: learning the culture, testing for misinformation introduced by distortions either of the self or the respondents, and building trust". As the present study took place over a two-year period, this constitutes prolonged engagement and thus "sufficient time". The technique of triangulation was also utilized to insure the findings were credible. During data triangulation, a piece of evidence was compared and crosschecked with other kinds of evidence.

## Guiding framework

I decided to use an overall guiding framework to guide the initial stage of the teacher reflection group meetings and journal writing. This framework arose out of my previous work with teacher groups and is grounded in the experiences of these groups (Farrell, 2007). However, I did not use it as a prescription but rather as a guide to help us get started while at the same time remain open to what the teachers wanted to continue, change, or invent new items as we went along during the period of reflection. As it turned out, we followed most of the framework outlined below. The theoretical framework utilized for the teacher reflection group had four core elements: *Create opportunities for reflection, Negotiate ground rules, Make provisions for time,* and *Build trust*. These core elements were not isolated but all connected as one built on the other and all need to be considered as a whole (see Farrell, 2007). I now briefly outline the five components of this framework.

### *Creating opportunities for reflection*

The first, and most important, component of the framework involves providing opportunities for language teachers to reflect through a range of approaches. These include exploring one's beliefs and classroom practices, classroom communication patterns and interaction, critical incidents, language proficiency, and teachers' metaphors and maxims. These were explored by such reflective tools as the use of group discussions, journal writing, and classroom observations. The teachers had the opportunity to use any of these reflective tools alone or used in combination with each other. For example, in the group reported on in this book writing in teaching journals assisted teachers to focus on specific aspects of their development, and these were used with classroom observations to document the teachers' beliefs. However, the classroom observations never really took off with the group mainly because of scheduling and they petered out after just a few. The use of the group meetings created the most opportunities for sustained concentration and discussion in which understandings of practice were constructed through talk. These discussions were recorded, transcribed, and later analysed for what issues occurred most frequently in discussions. The journals were also analysed. Providing these opportunities for teachers to reflect was only the first component of this model of reflection. In order to establish an atmosphere where reflective practice is encouraged, several conditions must be met. These conditions include the following: negotiated ground rules, providing for different types of time, and providing for a low affective state.

### Negotiating ground rules

The framework called for the group to negotiate a set of built-in rules or guidelines that the group and each teacher would agree to follow in order to focus their reflections over a period of time. For example, if teachers have decided to reflect with a group of teachers, they must consider who will chair the group meetings. One answer might be a different chairperson for each meeting with a resulting different level of responsibility (e.g. to provide a site and refreshments, and set the agenda and length of the meetings). However, as it turned out I as group facilitator chaired all of the meetings as the teachers agreed that this was the most comfortable way to conduct the meetings. That said, the teachers began to take more control after the fifth meeting (out of 13) when they became familiar with the routines of the discussion and my role was as a facilitator rather than a director. Of course, all of the above activities and built-in guidelines cannot be accomplished quickly; like all valuable things, they take time. This introduces the next important component of the model: *time.*

### Making time

For practicing teachers to be able to reflect on their work, time is a very important consideration and a very important commodity. I suggested that the teachers consider three different kinds of time and that they should define each type themselves before entering into the reflective process. These three are: individual time, activity time, and period of reflection time.

- *Individual time.* Practicing teachers are very busy in their daily teaching and other related duties, and the amount of time any one teacher is willing to invest in his or her professional self-development will naturally vary. This can create a dilemma for the group if all the participants do not attend all the group meetings or participate fully in the activities; group cohesion may be harmed. Therefore, a certain level of commitment by individual participants in terms of time availability should be negotiated by the group at the start of the process. All three teachers agreed to one semester of intense reflections (weekly group meetings) followed by another semester of less intense reflections (monthly group meetings) and then allowing themselves to be interviewed about their experiences and the findings from group meetings and journal writing over the following year.

- *Activity time.* Associated with the time each participant has to give to reflection is the time that should be considered when reflecting using specific activities. For example, for classroom observations, the number of times a class is to be observed should be negotiated ahead while also taking the first notion of time (individual) into consideration. The journal also needs time: time to write and time to read. Our group meetings turned out to be about two hours each in duration even though we initially agreed to one-hour meetings. Each teacher agreed to write as often as they could and although they agreed to frequent classroom observations, these did not occur with much frequency throughout the period of reflection.

- *Period of reflection time.* The final aspect of time concerns the time frame for the reflective period as a whole that teachers are willing to commit to. Teachers should consider how long they want to reflect. It is important to consider this for two reasons. When considering this aspect of time teachers should remember that critical reflection on one's teaching takes time, so the reflective period should be correspondingly long rather than short; otherwise, it might be time wasted. In addition, when teachers commit to having a fixed period in which to reflect, they also now know the exact period they can devote wholly to reflection.

### Building trust

The components of the framework on reflective language teaching outlined above all pose some threat and associated anxiety for practicing teachers when they engage in reflective teaching for any period of time. Therefore, a non-threatening environment should be encouraged by building up trust especially where peers and or groups are observing each other and involved in group discussions. Ways of establishing trust can be incorporated into the reflective process itself, such as emphasizing description and observation over judgment in classroom observations and group discussions. All three teachers knew each other before the group was formed and this helped ease any anxiety or tension. I as facilitator followed a position of listener rather than talker and although it took about five meetings for the group to really get going, trust was never really an issue through the whole reflective process. The first meeting was just talking about creating opportunities for reflection mentioned above as well as making the different provisions for time also mentioned above. After the first meeting the group discussion format generally followed a method of moving from chat (usually initiated by this author as facilitator in the first five meetings) to more focused discussions that were specific to the participants' work issues, details of which are presented in Chapter 4. When the group reflection period ended I consulted them informally (individually and on e-mail) about what I was writing but after the 13th formal group meeting, there were two more informal group meetings and lots of e-mail exchanges. I revisit the whole issue of setting up teacher reflection groups in Chapter 9 where I further explain what the teachers experienced within the group itself. I also provide recommendations for teachers wishing to set up some similar groups and that they can use a combination of the framework outlined above and the recommendations provided in Chapter 9.

## Moving forward with this book

*Reflective Practice in ESL Teacher Development Groups: From Practices To Principles* is written in a clear and accessible style and assumes no previous background in teacher education. Each chapter includes *Reflective Breaks* and tasks that prepare the reader to reflect on or apply the strategies or procedures discussed in the chapter. Teachers can gather as a group and reflect on the various topics the teachers discussed and consider the importance of these topics for their context. They can use these topics as a means of generating reflection into their own particular settings and then compare their findings with those reported on in this book.

## Outline of book

This introduction has outlined and discussed why this book is unique. The main reason for its uniqueness is that it takes a *Practice to Principles* approach to language teacher development and teacher expertise. This approach to teacher development and reflection explores the professional journeys and experiences of three experienced ESL teachers in Canada as relayed (through discussions, interviews, and journal writing and classroom observations) in their self-initiated teacher reflection group over a two-year period. The teacher reflection group followed an overall framework to guide the initial stage of the teacher reflection group meetings and journal writing that consisted of four core elements that all seemed to work well for the group: Create opportunities for reflection, Negotiate ground rules, Make provisions for time, and Build trust. This introductory chapter suggests that such a *Practice to Principles* approach to teacher development can give teachers, teacher educators, and administrators a realistic view of their worlds from their perspective and compare their views with what is being presented in current teacher education and development programs to see if these need change.

Chapter 1 discusses professional development of teachers and includes a discussion on teacher career cycles. The specific focus of the career cycle is teachers in mid-career years because all three teachers featured in the book are in mid-career (around the 15-year mark). The reason why teachers are encouraged to reflect in mid-career years (around the 15-year mark) is because they may be susceptible to the phenomenon known as "plateauing". "Plateauing" describes the frustration and disillusionment some teachers may experience over the course of their tenure in the classroom and that it usually happens to teachers in mid-career. The chapter notes that language teachers can become aware of the possibility of "plateauing" by engaging in systematic reflective inquiry (or evidence-based reflective practice) so that their enthusiasm for teaching can be sustained throughout their careers. The following chapter outlines how this can be achieved.

Chapter 2 outlines and discusses the concept of reflective practice (origins, definitions, principles and characteristics, and models of reflective practice) for language teachers. The chapter notes that reflective practice helps free the teachers from impulse and routine behavior because it allows teachers to act in a deliberate, intentional manner. Reflective practice involves systematically looking at what we do, how we do it, why we do it, what the outcomes are in terms of our student learning, and what actions we will take as a result of knowing all of this information. The chapter suggests that when language teachers engage in evidence-based systematic reflective practice by meeting regularly in a teacher reflection group, writing about their practice and examining their beliefs, roles and particular critical incidents they can become more aware of who they are and where they are going.

Chapter 3 outlines and discusses what three experienced ESL college teachers in Canada talked about in their group discussions as they reflected on their work over a period of time. The three most important topics were: school context, perceptions of self as teacher and learners. Embedded in these discussions were also more details about the role of the administration in institutions with ESL programs. In addition the group discussions were supportive as they were held in a non-threatening environment and all three teachers used the discussions to develop a new understanding of their practice as well as gain supportive feedback from peers. Such a group of teachers working together can achieve outcomes that would not be possible for an individual teacher working alone.

Chapter 4 outlines what the three teachers wrote about during the two-year reflective period. Writing is defined as a sit-down formal reflection time that could occur at any period during the reflective period and it was conducted on a computer. All three teachers seemed to use writing to focus more on their teaching approaches and activities than for the group discussions where they focused more generally on their school context. Perhaps this isolated act of writing can allow teachers more time to focus on teaching methods and group talk is more social and as such the working context in general would be more in focus. The chapter suggests that writing seems to be an effective means of facilitating reflection, and it has an added advantage in that it can be done alone or it can be shared with other teachers; however, if teachers share their reflection, they can attain different perspectives about their work as the results of this chapter have indicated.

Chapter 5 explores the sources of three experienced ESL teachers' beliefs in terms of the key influences on their teaching style. The main source of the three teachers teaching methods was their teaching personality and after reflecting on this, they can then consider if these chosen teaching methods really meet their students learning needs. Given that a teacher's teaching style involves the implementation of that teacher's philosophy about teaching, the chapter suggests that it is important for teachers to not only to become aware of their teaching styles but also what influences these (their beliefs) so that they can reflect on their relevancy for their current practice. When teachers are encouraged to articulate their beliefs and teaching style, they can become more confident practitioners, be more flexible about tolerating ambiguity and become more skilful in communicating to teachers, teacher educators, and administrators about issues related to their work.

Chapter 6 explores the three experienced ESL teachers' roles as revealed after scanning the group discussions and journal writing. A total of 16 main role identities were identified and divided into three major role identity clusters of teacher as manager, teacher as professional, and teacher as "acculturator", the latter of which may be somewhat unique to ESL teachers. The chapter suggests that when language teachers consciously reflect on the various roles (in terms of metaphors) they take on or are given to them by their institutions, colleagues, or others they can start the process of trying to figure out who they are and who they want to become as they continue their careers as reflective practitioners.

Chapter 7 explores critical incidents in the Teacher Reflection Group. The chapter suggests that language teachers can choose from various different means of imposing order on their seemingly disparate practices such as analysing critical incidents that occur in their practice and this can also cultivate the habit of engaging in reflective practice in general. The chapter uses a framework for analysing the narratives that the critical incidents emerged from as follows: Orientation, Complication, Evaluation, and Result. Two critical incidents were detailed in this chapter: Negative Feedback and Evaluation and Feedback from two of the teachers in the group.

Chapter 8 outlines and discusses how language teachers can consider their professional development through the lens of a teacher reflection group where they gather with a group of colleagues who may have perceived their career to be at a standstill so that they can learn how to understand, confront, and eventually resist plateauing. The chapter also discusses how teachers can cope and resist plateauing from the examples provided by the teachers such as collaborating with colleagues, enhancing their feelings of self-efficacy during the group discussions, and seeking out professional development opportunities to further develop themselves as teachers. The chapter outlines in detail how teachers can set up a teacher reflection group similar to the one presented in this book.

Chapter 9 outlines and discusses specific characteristics of ESL teacher expertise exhibited by the three teachers. The five main characteristics of teacher expertise identified were: Knowledge of Learners and Learning, Engage in Critical Reflection, Access Past Experiences, Informed Lesson Planning, and Active Student Involvement. In addition the teachers are constantly attempting to achieve a balance within and among the five main characteristics of teacher. It seems that teacher expertise is a process of becoming rather than reaching a state and that experience itself does not automatically translate into expertise. The three teachers presented in this book are not only expert ESL teachers but also caring professionals and a credit to the ELT profession.

# 1
# Professional Development

## Introduction

For many experienced teachers professional development invokes mixed feelings of hours or days spent at workshops, in-service courses experienced as part of (the usually mandated) professional development they are required to do at certain point in their careers. One of the reasons for the negative feelings that teachers experience with some professional development courses is because they have usually been mandated by the administration and the topics of these courses have also been decided by the same administrators. Many times, the teachers who are in the front lines of these institutions have not been consulted and as a result do not have any real commitment beyond attending. This type of professional development has often been called top-down professional development because it comes from above by the administrator, and its opposite if bottom-up professional development. Bottom-up professional development comes from below in that teachers are consulted and many times decide how and what they want to develop (Richards and Farrell, 2005). This bottom-up approach sees teachers are voluntary attendees and engage in professional development because they want to reflect on their practice in order to better serve their students. Teachers who engage in such professional development must also realize that to be successful they must also consider where they are in their overall career development or where they and what stage they are at on the teacher career cycle because teachers have different needs as they progress through the different career stages. This chapter discusses professional development for language teachers. This discussion includes the important concept of teachers' career cycles and the various stages and issues that teachers can experienced during the different stages they go through in their careers. The mid-career years are especially highlighted because of the main focus of the three experienced mid-career ESL teachers discussed throughout this book. The chapter then highlights the importance of language teachers of conducting their professional development through reflective practice.

## Professional development

There are many reasons for teachers to seek professional two of which concern teachers at different stages of their teaching career cycles: novice teachers who have just qualified and teachers in their mid-careers. For novice teachers even though they have just qualified after taking their initial teacher education programs there is now increasing realization by language teacher educators that their teacher learning and developing has only just begun. Many ELT scholars consider that the ever-expanding knowledge-base of second language teacher education cannot always be accounted for in these initial teacher education programs, and so teachers will need to consider professional development throughout their careers. So the first reason for teachers in their early career years to immediately consider their professional development is that they may not have in fact acquired all they need to know in their teacher education courses. In fact, there is still no agreement as to what should be offered in such programs, or how long such programs should be.

Another reason for teachers to consider development is that after years in the classroom they may need to reflect on their working principles and see where these have come from and how they have been shaped over the years. This type of development is especially important for teachers in their mid-career years because they have accumulated lots of various kinds of educational experiences and as such may need time to step back to consider their own personal professional development. Indeed, from the point of view of the teacher's personal development Richards and Farrell (2005: 9–10) maintain that a number of areas of personal professional development can be considered by teachers throughout their careers such as:

- *Subject-matter knowledge*: Increasing knowledge of the disciplinary basis of TESOL—that is, English grammar, discourse analysis, phonology, testing, second language acquisition research, methodology, curriculum development and the other areas which define the professional knowledge-base of language teaching.

- *Pedagogical expertise*: Mastery of new areas of teaching; adding to one's repertoire of teaching specializations; improving ability to teach different skill areas to learners of different ages and backgrounds
- *Self-awareness*: Knowledge of oneself as a teacher, of one's principles and values, strengths and weakness
- *Understanding of learners*: Deepening understanding of learners, learning styles, learners' problems and difficulties, ways of making content more accessible to learners
- *Understanding of curriculum and materials*: Deepening one's understanding of curriculum and curriculum alternatives, use and development of instructional materials
- *Career advancement*: Acquisition of the knowledge and expertise necessary for personal advancement and promotion, including supervisory and mentoring skills

So there are growing calls within the ELT profession for language teachers to regularly revisit what they know and what they think they know about teaching and learning and thus pursue various forms of professional development throughout their careers. Some of this professional development will be mandatory and delivered in a top-down manner while others types of professional development will be voluntary and undertaken by individual teachers in a bottom-up manner throughout their teacher career cycles (see below for more on career cycles).But what is professional development?

The term "professional development" has created a lot of discussion over the past 30 years in general education circles and there is still controversy as to its exact meaning. Much of the controversy surrounds the definition of development, what constitutes development and indeed, what teachers indent to obtain from development. For example, teacher development initiatives introduced before the 1990s were very linear in nature suggesting that teachers 'develop' in clearly defined, and fixed steps. It was suggested that teachers proceed through stages of development, and as Burden (1990) noted, transitions between stages were frequently viewed as relatively irreversible. However, Bell and Gilbert (1994: 311) opposed this view of teacher development and maintained that teacher development is in fact teachers learning about and "developing their beliefs and ideas, developing their classroom practice, and attending to their feelings associated with changing." They said that teachers in development are actually learning about how they learn themselves. Furthermore, Bell and Gilbert (1994) suggested that the purpose of such an approach to teacher development is to empower teachers for ongoing and continuous development, rather than passing through any fixed steps or stages.

## Reflective questions

- What does professional development mean to you?
- Do you think teachers follow defined stages or phases in their careers?
- Before reading about teacher career cycles below, what stage or phase of your career do you think you are in now and why?
- Describe your particular phase or stage?
- Have you ever felt that you have plateaued yet or gone a little stale in your teaching career?
- If yes, describe your feelings and what you think has lead up to these feelings.

Regardless of which definition of teacher development one adheres to, Burden (1990) maintains that in order to understand teacher development, it is important to understand the interaction of physical, psychological, and social aspects of human development. In other words, teacher development should be included in the broader context of adult development. Early recognition of the relationship between adult development and teacher development came from Sprinthall and Thies-Sprinthall (1980) and Burden (1990). Sprinthall and Thies-Sprinthall (1980) for example, asserted that consideration in any training model (however, see below for definition of "training" as opposed to "development") of teachers should be given to the teacher as adult learner. Also, Burden (1990: 325) pointed out that when designing programs to promote teacher development, "it is important to recognize how adults learn, how they prefer to learn, and what they want to learn." However, more recently, Cooper and Boyd (1998: 58–59) have maintained that traditional models of staff development often ignore principles of adult learning, where adult development is linked to their self-worth and efficacy. They suggest that adults in such a program learn through active involvement following such principles as:

1. Opportunities to try out new practice and be self-directed in the learning process.
2. Careful and continuous guided reflection and discussion about proposed changes and time to analyze one's own experience, since experience is the richest source of adult learning.

3. Personal support for participants during the change process.
4. Provisions for differences in style, time, and pace of learning.

## Reflective questions

* Why do you think staff development (in-service) programs tend to ignore principles of adult learning outlined above?
* When taking an adult learning approach to teacher development, which methods and procedures should be made available to teachers in an in-service program?

It is important at this juncture to emphasize that different terms such as teacher education, training and development have different meanings and involve different emphasizes for teachers. For example, the terms *training, preparation, education,* and *development* have been used very loosely in the literature when discussing the preparation and development of teachers for the classroom (Lange, 1990). Lange (1990) suggests that he first two are somewhat unsatisfactory because he says 'preparation' suggests an idea of supplying future teachers' needs before they really begin their work but this does not necessarily suggest helping them to continue their development throughout their whole careers. In addition, Lange (1990) maintains that the term "training" suggests a misleading sense of completeness in the preparation of teachers whereas as the term "development" connotes more of a continuance. In second language education the term "development" suggests that teachers be prepared to be able to make their own informed decisions about teaching well beyond the initial teacher education course (Richards and Farrell, 2005).

## Training

It is important to note that when teacher educators put an emphasis on *training,* they are looking for learner teachers to be able to isolate, practice, and eventually master discrete teaching behaviors such as teacher talk, wait time, and use of questioning techniques. As Freeman (1982: 21) notes, in such training approach "the teacher learns to teach the same way as I learn to ride a bicycle." Wallace (1991) has called the training approach the "craft model" of teaching in which the master teacher tells the students what to do, and shows them how to do it, with the students imitating it exactly. Within this craft model of teaching, the teacher educator's role will be that of direct intervention to transmit the required, "correct" knowledge and skills to the dependent pre-service teacher. Some teachers, especially inexperienced, pre-service teachers, like this approach because of their own insecurity; they see supervisors as authority figures and looks to them for security and advice. For in-service teachers, a training approach would assume that supervisors/leaders would know (experts) what good teaching is and participating teachers would have to change their teaching behavior to meet the expectations of the supervisors/leaders. However, a training view of teaching leaves second language education at the level of knowledge and skill; knowledge in the form of what is being taught, to whom and where; skill, the basic component, in what to do in the classroom (give instructions, present materials). The training model is also limited by the fact that we still do not know exactly what the cause–effect of teaching to learning outcomes is; not enough is known about how teaching behaviors result in student learning.

### Development

In the 1990s within the second language teacher education literature there was a move away from a training approach to a development approach. Although we can talk about the craft of teaching, such as checking attendance, we cannot really say exactly what the "art" of teaching entails. However, a developmental view of teaching recognizes this "art" aspect of teaching as well as the craft of teaching, recognizing professional development as a continual intellectual, experiential, and attitudinal growth of teachers. In this approach, the role of teacher educators, supervisors, and workshop leaders changes from a prescriptive type leadership (training) to providing opportunities for teachers to participate in a variety of activities (Farrell, 2013). These opportunities can be subsumed under a reflective practice approach to teacher development. This bottom-up approach to teacher development involves a reflective analysis of a teacher's practices and will be the main focus of the contents of this book. Reflection in this approach is viewed as a process whereby teachers examine their beliefs and practices about teaching and learning so that they can better understand these beliefs and practices.

Thus because of the expanding knowledge-base of second language teaching, it has been suggested that language teachers today are more in need of some sort of professional development not because they have been inadequately trained but as Richards and Farrell (2005) have suggested, because they cannot possibly be taught everything they need to know at the pre-service level of training and education. Indeed, it is also a given now that language teachers will have different needs at different times during their teaching careers depending on what phase of their career cycle they are located.

## Teacher career cycles

It is well known that all teachers go through certain stages or phases during their careers and there have been many influential scholars who have examined these phases over the years, however, they do not always agree of the nature of these phases. As an example, I will briefly compare just four influential studies (two at the pre-service level and two at the in-service level) first because these are the basis for one of the models that I will emphasize in this chapter. Table 1.1 compares four studies: two on pre-service teacher development and two on in-service teacher development.

Table 1.1 illustrates different models of development and suggests that pre-service teachers appear to experience different concerns while developing as teachers. For example, Fuller and Brown's (1975) classic model illustrates a development sequence of concerns for pre-service teachers. In the first phase, called pre-teaching concerns, pre-service teachers identify realistically with students but only in fantasy with the role of teachers. They do not see teaching realistically. In the second stage, there are early concerns about survival. Teachers' idealized concerns are replaced by concerns about their own survival as teachers. They are also concerned about control of the class and the content of their instruction. In the third stage, teachers become concerned about their teaching performance, including the limitations and frustrations of the teaching situation. In the fourth stage, teachers become more concerned about

*Table 1.1* Pre-service and in-service teachers' development stages

| Pre-service | | In-service | |
| --- | --- | --- | --- |
| **Fuller and Brown (1975)** | **Caurso (1977)** | **Katz (1972)** | **MacDonald (1982)** |
| Pre-teaching concerns | Anxiety/euphoria | Survival | Transition |
| Early survival concerns | Confusion/clarity | Consolidation | Exploring |
| Teaching concerns | Competence/inadequacy | Renewal | Invention |
| Student concerns | Criticism/awareness | Maturity | Professional |

*Source*: Adapted from Bruden (1990).

their students' learning. In contrast, Caruso (1977) identified phases of feelings that student teachers had about themselves and about their experiences as they were teaching. He said that these phases were not mutually exclusive and that there was much overlap. He gave labels to these phases: (a) anxiety/euphoria, (b) confusion/clarity, (c) competence/ inadequacy, and (d) criticism/new awareness.

For in-service teachers' stages of development, Katz (1972) suggested four developmental stages for the professional growth of teachers. He said that the length of time a teacher stays in each stage will vary. In the first stage, the survival stage, teachers are concerned about surviving as they realize the differences between their anticipated success and the reality of the classroom. In stage two, the consolidation stage, teachers try to consolidate the gains made in the first stage, while they also begin to focus on individual students, and on specific tasks to be accomplished. In stage three, the renewal stage, teachers look for innovations in their field. In the fourth stage, teachers try to come to terms with themselves as teachers. They begin to ask deeper and more abstract questions about teaching. McDonald (1982) also suggests four stages of professional growth for in-service teachers. In the first stage, the transition stage as he calls it, teachers learn the basic skills of managing and organizing their class. They then begin to explore in the second stage now that they have these basic skills. In stage three, teachers start to invent and experiment with their teaching techniques. In stage four, the professional teaching stage, teachers develop problem-solving skills and in turn may be able to help other teachers to be creative.

## Reflective questions

- Why would pre-service teachers pass through different phases than in-service teachers?
- Which of the models above do you support and why?
- Did and do you go through different phases smoothly or do you think you go through more than one phase at the same time?
- Do you think teachers can return to a phase they have experienced at an early time of their teaching career?

## Huberman's model

Clearly, there are many different approaches to the study of teacher development as related to teacher lifecycles and all of these have laid an important groundwork and base for more recent and more extensively researched model of teacher life cycles by Michael Huberman (1989, 1993). The main change in thinking about a teacher's career cycle by scholars after the important early groundbreaking studies outlined in the section above was that teachers, rather than moving neatly through set phases or stages, were now seen as moving in and out of phases in response to environmental influences from both personal and institutional pressures and challenges.

Michael Huberman's (1989) classic research on the professional life-cycle of teachers has revealed that teachers pass through different phases in their career, from novice (early, mid, late novice), to mid-career (stabilization, experimentation, taking stock) to late-career (serenity, disengagement). Knowledge of this cycle is important for educators because it explains that a teacher's progression through his or her career cycle is filled with "plateaus, discontinuities, regressions, spurts, and dead ends" (Huberman, 1995: 196).

In terms of years of teaching experience, the model charts that one to three years teaching experience, called the novice years, are characterized by the novice teacher's primary concern of surviving in a new environment. This is then followed by a period of discovery of the act of teaching and its impact on student learning. Year four to year six as a teacher follow and are characterized by some stabilization where teachers have committed somewhat to the profession and begin to experience as Huberman (1989: 34) suggests, "greater instructional master and comfort, a more assertive professional autonomy." Teachers are now more experienced and feel more confident about their teaching skills and follow a comfortable professional pattern inside and outside the classroom. Some teachers may even begin to experiment with new approaches and activities in order to make their teaching more interesting or exciting. In mid-career, Huberman (1989) maintains that some teachers may also begin to take stock of their careers and reflect on their past and future as teachers. Beyond these years, teachers can find job satisfaction or not. For those who do find satisfaction, they become content and eventually retire feeling fulfilled. For those who do not find job satisfaction, they become disengaged and retire felling bitter. The above phases are not linear and teachers tend to move into and out of different stages at different times during their careers; rather as Fessler and Christensen (1992: 42) have noted, there is "a dynamic ebb and flow, where teachers move in and out of stages in response to influences from personal and organizational dimensions." In other words, teachers can bypass a certain phase or revert to a phase undergone earlier in their career.

## Mid-career years

Awareness of the stage or phase a teacher is on along the professional life cycle is important for a teacher's professional development because as Downey, Steffy, English, Frase, and Poston (2004: 175) have noted: "Professional development that is effective for beginning teachers is far different from that which is effective for teachers at other points in their careers."

The focus of this study reported on in this book is the mid-career stage or phase (7–18 years of teaching experience on the model) as all participants are mid-career teachers (see section on participants below). At the mid-career stage, Huberman (1989: 43) maintains that some teachers begin to notice a shift in their thinking to where they "feel the stale breath of routine" and as a result can drift to the "problematic" right side of the model representing a trajectory of *Stocktaking/interrogations* as teachers begin to experience self-doubt and thus become susceptible to the phenomenon of "plateauing" (Milstein, 1990). Plateauing, according to Milstein (1990: 325), can occur if teachers perceive that their work has become so routine and repetitive that they "become skeptical about ever finding fulfillment in our careers." One factor that can lead to teachers experiencing plateauing is the very nature of the teaching profession: because teaching is considered a "front-loaded" job (Lortie, 1975). It is "front-loaded" in the sense that most teachers achieve professional privileges on entry or very early into the professional lives; however, these privileges do not improve significantly throughout a teacher's career. So the longer they remain as teachers, the more likely they are to experience some form of plateauing (see Chapter 8 for more on plateauing).

Within language teaching Tsui (2003: 80) also maintains that after several years of teaching, teachers can begin to experience self-doubt that can be caused by such factors as the "monotony of classroom teaching, and unpleasant working conditions." So an important question is how can teachers become aware of the real possibility of the phenomenon of plateauing so that their enthusiasm for teaching can be maintained throughout their careers. Meister and Ahrens (2011) report that one way of making teachers aware of such issues in mid-career is to encourage them to engage in collaborative reflections in teacher reflection groups. Meister and Ahrens's (2011) research discovered that when teachers have an opportunity to explore teaching through informal group talk, they learn from each. Meister and Ahrens (2011: 777) further reported that the group discussions helped to "break their feelings of isolation" and also provided them with "the support they needed to overcome their problems." Within ELT, Kiely and Davis (2010: 278) have also noted that the development of experienced language teachers "is effectively supported by collaborative processes where teachers share experiences and jointly explore ways of changing their practice."

## Reflective questions

- Why (and how) could a teacher find himself or herself drifting to the "problematic" right side of the model representing a trajectory of *Stocktaking/interrogations*?
- Have you ever experienced self-doubt?
- How can experiences of self-doubt lead a teacher to become susceptible to the phenomenon of "plateauing"?
- Do you think that reflecting on practice could help teachers deal with self-doubt about their teaching?
- If yes, how? If no, why not?

## Reflective practice

Reflective practice as a term is not a new phenomenon in today's literature on professional development; however, the question of what reflective practice is (definition), what it involves and how to implement reflective practice still remains open to question in the general education literature as well as second language education (if not more so within the field of second language education (see Farrell, 2013 for example). The fact that the debate about what reflective practice is and what it entails remains open is not a bad thing because it means that teachers themselves will still have define it and decide what aspects of reflective practice they may want to use for their needs. This is good because it also means reflective practice has still not been reduced to a method where teachers can mindlessly plug in to see what they can get out of it—something like a blind adherence to a particular teaching method where a teacher routinely plugs without really looking at the needs of the students who will feel the impact of the method. Consequently, teachers should as Jay and Johnson (2002: 73) maintain, try to "clarify [his or her own] understanding of reflection so it can be made personally meaningful."

The great American educator, John Dewey warned teachers against blindly following routing in their thinking and in their teaching because routine actions may not be the actions you want or need. Dewey (1933) said that when teachers follow routine actions (and thinking) in their classes it may be because of the ideas of a persuasive colleague or because of the bureaucracy of the school in which one teaches in (i.e., you *will* do this in class), or worse, your own impulse with a last minute decision about what and how to teach something. For Dewey (1933) who was working in a post-depression United States, the aim of any education was to encourage students (and teachers) to engage in intelligent thought and action, not routine thought and action. Freedom from routine according to Dewey (1933) could be obtained if teachers engaged in reflective inquiry. Dewey viewed reflective inquiry as "active, persistent, and careful consideration of any belief or supposed form of knowledge in the light of the grounds that support it and the further conclusions to which it tends [that] constitutes reflective thought" (Dewey 1933: 3–16).

I should say that Dewey's idea of reflective inquiry has influenced a lot of the contents of this book because it suggests that teachers can act in a deliberate and intentional manner about what we teach our students. In other words, we should not allow others (be they from within our outside our institutions or schools) to tell us what to do or what way we should teach. Rather we should determine for ourselves what and how we should teach but not in an impulsive manner and not just mulling over things before or after class in what some have called "navel gazing." We should actively look at what we do for experience as a teacher in itself is not enough for learning if we do not reflect on that experience. As Dewey (1933) recommended, teachers should combine actual teaching experiences with genuine systematic reflections (and not "navel gazing") so that we can become more aware of our practices. I call this evidence-based reflective practice.

## Reflective questions

- What is reflective teaching?
- Should teachers reflect? Why or why not?
- What are the benefits of reflective practice?
- How should teachers reflect?
- Should teachers follow routine? Why or why not?

### Reflective inquiry

Dewey (1933: 35) observed that teachers who do not bother to think intelligently about their work become slaves to this routine, and he noted that one of the main challenges of learning was learning how to think intelligently; as he observed: "While we cannot learn or be taught to think, we do have to learn how to think well, especially how to acquire the general habits of reflecting." Some may say that routine is necessary but when I was asked recently how I teach the same classes each year, I answered that I do not teach "classes" I teach students do there is no routine for me; it all depends how each student reacts or does not react. So Dewey is correct to suggest that teachers should be on guard against blindly following routine because if we do this, then we will certainly be teaching classes rather than students. This to me is a form of reflective thinking.

For Dewey, the cause of reflective thinking comes out of the feeling of doubt or conflict connected to teaching. He then mapped out five main phases of reflective thought that he considered not in a particular order but rather were fluid:

1. *Suggestion*: A doubtful situation is understood to have being problematic and some vague suggestions are considered as possible solutions. Let us say a group of international students have been dropping out of class suddenly and we wonder what we can do about it.
2. *Intellectualization*: An intellectualization of the difficulty or perplexity of the problem that has been felt (directly experienced) into a problem to be solved. We begin to wonder if they have any difficulties with their study, or finance, or travel or even culture differences.
3. *Guiding Idea*: The use of one suggestion after another as a leading idea, or hypothesis; the initial suggestion can be used as a working hypothesis to initiate and guide observation and other operations in the collection of factual material. So we research our teachers and ask their opinion about what is going on and we also research the students themselves to see if they have any specific problems such as financial problems with their ability to pay course fees and the like, or cultural problems fitting in to study in a new country and education system and so on.
4. *Reasoning*: Reasoning link present and past ideas and help elaborate the supposition reflective inquiry has reached or the mental elaboration of the idea or supposition as an idea or supposition. As we begin to try to solve the problem we consider giving college-wide financial scholarships to those international students in need or find other solutions.
5. *Hypothesis testing*: The refined idea is reached and the testing of this refined hypothesis takes place; the testing can be by overt action or in thought (imaginative action). We make some plan of action about

our international students and we monitor it closely to see if it has a positive impact on international student retention.

## Reflective questions

- Use Dewey's five stages of reflective inquiry above and go through an issue/problem that you have had to deal with recently in your practice.
- Did you want to jump to finding a quick answer to your issue/problem and not go through each step? Why or why not?
- Did you find it easy or difficult to suspend your thoughts and go through each stage? Why or why not?

This was the first real systematization of reflective inquiry into teaching that I can remember seeing in the literature and it is structured to suggest that teachers look at their experiences, review, and examine these in light of what evidence they can collect from their practice and then plan what action they want to take as a result. Interested readers may want to note that Boud, Keogh, and Walker (1985) have since built on the work of Dewey and suggested a cyclical model with three broader categories of reflective thought (*experience, reflection,* and *outcome*) that emphasize emotion as an element of reflective practice. In addition, Zeichner and Liston (1987: 24) also returned to Dewey's original ideas when they distinguished between routine action and reflective action and suggested that for teachers "routine action is guided primarily by tradition, external authority and circumstance" whereas reflective action "entails the active, persistent and careful consideration of any belief or supposed form of knowledge."

## Conclusion

This chapter has outlined and discussed professional development for teachers and also the importance of teachers in mid-career years to engage in reflective practice as part of their professional development. The reason why teachers are encouraged to reflect in mid-career years is because they may be susceptible to the phenomenon known as "plateauing." "Plateauing" describes the frustration and disillusionment some teachers may experience over the course of their tenure in the classroom and that it usually happens to teachers in mid-career. This may because at this stage of their teaching life, their work may seem to be routine repetitive, and some may feel that they have lost their bearings in terms of career fulfillment. The chapter notes that language teachers can become aware of the possibility of "plateauing" by engaging in systematic reflective inquiry (or *evidence-based reflective practice*) so that their enthusiasm for teaching can be sustained throughout their careers. The following chapter outlines how this can be achieved.

# 2
# Reflective Practice

## Introduction

Recently within TESOL teachers have been encouraged to reflect on their practice as part of their own professional development (Garton and Richards, 2008; Farrell, 2007; Richards and Farrell, 2005). This reflective process really means that teachers consciously examine what they believe about their practice or as Mann (2005: 105) has suggested, articulating "an inner world of choices made in response to the outer world of the teaching context." They then compare these beliefs to their actual classroom practices to see if there is convergence or divergence. In other words, by articulating their beliefs, assumptions and values about teaching and learning, and comparing these to what they do in the classroom, teachers can become more aware of what they think and do so that they can make informed decisions about their practice. This type of reflection on practice also allows practicing teachers to take more responsibility for their actions. It is especially important for experienced teachers to be able to give accounts about their existing beliefs, assumptions, values, and knowledge concerning their work so that they can be acknowledged as professionals similar to other fields such a medicine or law. It is also important to be able to include these personal conceptualizations of what it means to teach English to speakers of other language within the ever-expanding knowledge base of second language teacher education and development so that those new to the profession can benefit from their experiences. Thus, one of the purposes of this book is to obtain the reflections of English language teachers who are in mid-career so that all teachers of English as a second or foreign language can benefit from knowledge of their experiences reflecting on their practice over a two-year period. But what is reflective practice and what does it entail? There is general agreement among scholars both in general education and TESOL that some form of reflection is desirable but that is where the agreement stops as there is still no agreement on the definition of reflection or reflective practice. I do not think that this lack of clarity at the scholar level about what reflection is or what it entails is a bad thing because it also means that individual teachers and teacher reflection groups must decide for themselves what their idea and definitions of reflection entail for them. In other words, they must reflect on reflective practice rather than just implement some methodology of reflection developed by others without any real understanding of what this all means for them. This chapter outlines and discusses what reflective practice is, and also gives details of the various modes of reflection that the teacher reflection group reported on in this book utilized as they reflected on their practice over the two-year period so that other teachers and teacher groups can consider not only the topics/issues that were reflected on within mode (and through the specific reflective questions that accompany each topic), but also to consider if they want to emulate some or all of these modes as they reflect on their own practice.

## Reflective questions

- What does reflective practice mean to you?
- Why do you think there is not much scholarly agreement on what reflective practice means?
- Should language teachers reflect on their practice?
- How can teachers reflect?
- What kind of information can teachers get when they reflect on their practice?
- What are the greatest barriers for teachers wishing to reflect on their practice?

## Reflective practice

Reflecting on practice generally means that teachers subject their own beliefs, assumptions, and values about the teaching and learning to a critical analysis (Farrell, 2007, 2013). Of course, there have been many different definitions of reflective practice written over the years (I counted over 100 different definitions over the past 20 years); some consider it just "mulling over" things before and after classes while sitting in a bus/subway car or the like, while others consider it a more rigorous examination of practice where teachers engage in some systematic exploration of their practices. The former view of reflection where teachers informally explore their practice in non-systematic ways is a good start because at least they are thinking about what they do and it may be a necessary starting point to more formal reflections. In fact, it is safe to say that all teachers engage in this type of "reflection" at some point in their teaching lives and this is for sure when they are in the classroom and they are monitoring how their lesson is going, or at least how they perceive it is going. I use the work "perceive" because what they think is happening in their classroom and what is actually happening may not be the same. In my experience teachers who only engage in such unstructured reflection may actually end up frustrated because they may become overwhelmed with the amount of information that they encounter before, during and after lessons. This type of informal reflection actually does not really lead to improved teaching and can even lead to more "unpleasant emotions without suggesting any way forward" (Wallace, 1991: 13). Furthermore, we may become too hard on ourselves and only reflect on problems that occur rather than also reflecting on what we do well. So, while informal reflections on our practice may be a necessary beginning to our overall development as language teachers, it can have undesirable consequences if we do not take it further and systematically explore our practice through structured reflections.

Thus, the latter definition of reflective practice discussed above, sometimes called "evidence-based" reflective practice, suggests that language teachers systematically examine their practice by collecting evidence about their own teaching and their students' learning rather than just thinking about what they may be doing in their classes. This type of reflective practice takes the pressure off teachers in the sense that they will not experience cognitive overload trying to perceive what they do without any real evidence that this is true or not. With evidence-based reflective practice teachers can use the evidence they gather about their practice to make decisions about their teaching and their students' learning but these are no longer the "usual" or "routine" decisions they make. Indeed, the great American educator John Dewey (1933: 17) considered reflection a form of freedom from routine behavior: "reflection emancipates us from merely impulsive and merely routine activity, it enables us to direct our activities with foresight and to plan according to ends-in-view or purposes of that we are aware, to act in deliberate and intentional fashion, to know what we are about when we act." In this sense he encouraged teachers (and all citizens really) to make informed decisions about their teaching and that these decisions be based on systematic and conscious reflections rather than fleeting thoughts about teaching. Dewey maintained that when teachers combined these systematic reflections with their actual teaching experiences, then they could become more aware and this would lead to professional development and growth as a teacher. Thus Dewey was advocating early for a form of evidence-based teaching.

An evidence-based approach to reflective practice suggests that teacher can become informed decisions about practice: informed from evidence gathered rather than perceptions that may or may not be correct (Farrell, 2007, 2013). This informed, rather than routine, decision-making process is based on systematic and conscious reflections because now a teacher's teaching experience is also combined with systematic reflections on practice, thus leading to greater overall awareness of the teaching learning process. Such evidence-based reflective practice also leads to a teacher's overall development and growth. The contents of this book are derived from such an evidence-based approach to reflective practice.

## Reflective questions

- Do you follow routine when you teach?
- Do you think routine action is guided by tradition, external authority, or some other event?
- If yes, what form of tradition, who is the external authority and what is the circumstance?
- What are your particular classroom routines when you are teaching?
- Do you start/end a class in the same way all the time?
- Do you think routine is necessary for teachers?
- Do you think routine is necessary for students?
- Do you think reflection can emancipate us from impulsive and routine activity in our teaching? If yes, how? If not, why not?
- Dewey suggested that with systematic reflections teachers can become more aware and this awareness would lead to professional development and growth as a teacher. How can teachers achieve this development and growth?
- What is the difference between evidence-based reflective practice and routine reflections on practice?
- How can a teacher engage in evidence-based reflective practice?

In the previous section, the focus of reflective practice suggests that teachers move away from routine teaching and engage in reflective teaching. Much of the early work on reflective practice originated from John Dewey in the 1930s but there was a bit of a lull for many years after Dewey's revolutionary thoughts on teaching and reflection until the 1980s with the work of Donald Schön (1983, 1987). I am not saying that teachers did not reflect during those years but within the literature on education and teaching not many scholars took up the mantel of reflective practice until the work of Donald Schön in the 1980s. Some scholars say that imprints of John Dewey's work are ever present in the work of Donald Schön. In fact, Schön focused his dissertation on Dewey's *Theory of Inquiry* and many say that this focus gave his views on reflection more of a pragmatic framework (than many even today who are overly theoretical) that was present in most of his later work. Although Schön was interested in many aspects of organizational behavior, it is probably safe to say that for educators his work centered on the notion of practitioner-generated intuitive practice or what teachers do in class without thinking too much about it because he suggested that teachers may not be able to articulate what they do or at least they know more than they can articulate about their practice.

Schön (1983: vii) made this clear in his early influential book, *The Reflective Practitioner: How Professionals Think in Action*, when he said: "We are in need of inquiry into the epistemology of practice. What is the kind of knowing in which competent practitioners engage? How is professional knowing like and unlike the kinds of knowing in academic textbooks, scientific papers and journals?" In the 1970s Schön first teamed up with Chris Argris and developed the notion of single-loop and double-loop learning (Argyris and Schön, 1974). Single-loop learning is defined as planning, teaching, and testing but as they noted this remains at the tacit level of learning whereas double-loop learning is where thinking, practice, and problems between the two are raised to an explicit level where they can be accessed.

Most of all however, Schön was very interested in how professionals "know" through their practice because he was convinced they know more than they articulate into language. This he called *reflection-in-action*, or how teachers think on their feet. Reflection-in-action involves examining our beliefs and experiences and how they connect to our theories-in-use. However, in order to engage in reflection-in-action we must become aware of our *knowing-in-action* and this process moves beyond the usual established ideas as practitioners build up and draw on a collection of images, ideas, and actions. Applying Schön's work to teaching (although he did not write directly about teachers in his seminal book), knowing-in-action would be crucial because teachers cannot possibly question every action or reaction while they are teaching otherwise they would not be able to get through a class.

So a teacher's knowing-in-action works similar to when we recognize a face in a crowd but we do not list or try to consciously piece together each separate facial feature that makes a person recognizable to us. We do not consciously think, "Could that be ... ?" —we just know. In addition, if you were asked to describe the features that prompted this recognition, it might be difficult because, as Schön (1983) has pointed out, that type of information usually remains at the subconscious level of our thoughts. However, when a new situation or event occurs and our established routines do not work for us, then according to Schön (1983), teachers use reflection-in-action to cope. Reflection-in-action involves a reflective conversation where the practitioner is listening to the "situations' backtalk." Thus there is a sequence of moments in a process of reflection-in-action in which the practitioner attempts to solve a problem as follows:

• A situation develops which triggers spontaneous, routine responses (such as in knowing-in-action): For example, a student cannot answer an easy grammar question that he or she was able to during the previous class such as identifying a grammar structure.
• Routine responses by the teacher (i.e. what the teacher has always done) do not produce a routine response and instead produce a surprise for the teacher: The teacher starts to explain how the student had already explained this grammar structure in the previous class and so the teacher wonders why this is the case. The teacher asks the student if anything is the matter and the student says he forgets the answer.
• This surprise response gets the teacher's attention and leads to reflection within an action: The teacher reacts quickly to try to find out why the student suddenly "forgets" a grammar structure the teacher knows the student has no trouble understanding. The teacher can ask the student directly to explain what is happening.
• Reflection now gives rise to on-the-spot experimentation by the teacher: The student may or may not explain why he or she is crying. The teacher will take some measures (depending on the reaction or non-reaction) to help solve the problem: ignore the situation, empathize with the student, help the student answer the question by modeling answers, and so forth.

According to Schön these sequences of moments are all present and lead to reflection-in-action. In this case, Schön says that practitioners engage in a process of problem setting rather than problem-solving. As Clarke (1995: 245) explains: "This conversation between the practitioner and the setting provides the data which may then lead to new meanings, further reframing, and plans for further action."

## Reflective questions

- What does reflection-in-action mean to you?
- What is a teacher's knowing-in-action?
- How can a teacher listen to a situation in teaching "backtalk"?
- Why would a teacher know more about teaching than he or she can articulate?

Dewey (1933) considered reflective practice as intentional, systematic inquiry that was disciplined and that would ultimately lead to change and professional growth for teachers (reflecting-*on*-action). Schön added to this the idea of a practitioner being able to reflect on his or her intuitive knowledge while engaged in the action of teaching (or reflecting-*in*-action). We can also add the idea that both types of reflection: *in* and *on* action, can encourage teachers to reflect-*for*-action. Their legacy is important because they moved the concept of reflection far beyond everyday simple wonderings about a situation to a more rigorous form of thinking where a teacher systematically investigates a perceived "problem" in order to discover a solution. That said, Dewey (1933) did not consider a problem as an error or a mistake but rather a puzzling, curious, inviting, and engaging issue for a teacher to investigate. Like Dewey I consider reflective practice as a form of systematic inquiry that is rigorous and disciplined and like Schön I am interested in how teachers "think on their feet" or how they reflect in action, on action, and for action.

For me the implications of both Dewey and Schön's work is that reflective teaching is evidence-based where teachers collect data or evidence about their work, and then reflect on this evidence to make informed decisions about their practice. Engaging in evidence-based reflective practice allows teachers to articulate to themselves (and others) what they do, how they do it, why they do it, and what the impact of one's teaching is on student learning. This type of articulation is what Schön was talking about. The results of engaging in such reflective practice may mean an affirmation of current practices or making changes, but these changes will not be based on impulse, tradition or the like, but as a result of analysis of concrete evidence.

In addition, both Dewey and Schön's work suggest that teachers can look at what is actual and occurring (theories-in-use) in their practice and compare this to their beliefs (espoused theories) about learning and teaching. This productive tension (Freeman, personal communication) between "espoused theories" and "theories-in-use" provide teachers with the opportunity to systematically look at their practice so that they can deepen their understanding of what they do and thus come to new insights about their students, their teaching, and themselves. As Dewey (1933: 87) noted, growth comes from a "reconstruction of experience," and by reflecting on these experiences we can reconstruct our own approaches to teaching. There are different modes of reflection that teachers can consider to investigate their practice some of which include teacher reflection groups where teachers explore their beliefs, assumptions, and values about their practice in a safe environment. Within this group setting, teachers can talk, and write about their beliefs and practice as well as engage in classroom observations to compare their beliefs and practices.

## Reflective questions

- Why is it important for a teacher to reconstruct teaching experiences?
- How can a teacher reconstruct experience?
- Think of a puzzling, curious, inviting, and engaging issue that occurred in your teaching and try to investigate it.

## Teacher reflection group

One way experienced language teachers can engage in evidence-based reflections on their work is to encourage them to form a teacher reflection group (Farrell, 2007). Reflective practice involves teachers engaging in "a dialogue of thinking and doing" (Schön, 1983: 31), and this may be best accomplished in the company of other teachers in a teacher reflection group (Humaira and Rarieya, 2008). It is important for experienced language teachers to talk about their career experiences because as Garton and Richards (2008: p. xxii) have noted, "the way teachers talk about their experiences is fundamental to understanding how a teacher's knowledge influences what happens in the context of their work, and is in turn, influenced by what happens there."

A teacher reflection group can be defined as "any form of co-operative and ongoing arrangement between two or more teachers to work together on their own personal and professional development" (Head and Taylor, 1997: 91). Teacher reflection groups involve teachers as Humaira and Rarieya (2008: 270) point out, "undertaking an inquiry into their practice through verbally sharing, discussing, questioning and reasoning about their teaching experiences, either with their peers and/ or a reflective coach. " So, when teachers reflect with other teachers, they can "look back on events, make judgments about them, and alter their teaching behaviors in light of craft, research, and ethical knowledge" (Valli, 1997: 70).

Richards and Farrell (2005) maintain that language teachers come together in such groups on the basic assumption that collaborating with a group of colleagues will be more effective than reflecting alone, and as a result of participating in teacher development groups, teachers can change their thinking about their work and as a result can become more confident language teachers (Matlin and Short, 1991). This is because language teacher reflection groups facilitate dialogue, sharing, and collaboration and the exchange of resources, information, and expertise that may not be possible if teachers reflect alone (Richards and Farrell, 2005). When these reflective conversations are based on shared teaching practices and experiences they can provide opportunities for the "deconstruction of those experiences and the reconstruction of a shared meaning in a way that transforms understandings and changes practice" (Crow and Smith, 2005: 491). In addition, reflective conversations provide teachers with opportunities to look back on events and practices so that they can as Humaira and Rarieya (2008: 270) suggest, "Make an important contribution to building a shared repertoire of skills and techniques amongst teachers and educators in a school."

Meister and Ahrens (2011) suggest that these groups should be teacher-initiated support groups rather than contrived collegiality that can originate in top-down mandates, as these can be the catalyst for achieving teacher renewal. This was also the case for the teacher reflection group reported on in this book because when teachers have the opportunity to explore teaching in group talk in a teacher reflection group, they can learn from each other in the group setting and also obtain support from each other to systematically look at their practice together in a safe environment (see Chapter 3 for more).

In order to help them reflect on their practice they also decided to write regularly about their practice in a teaching journal. Writing is another tool for reflection because it enables teachers to step back from their thoughts after they have put them in writing so that they can deliberate intentionally and carefully on what they are thinking. In other words, the act of writing has its own built-in stoppage because not only must teachers consciously consider what they will write about but also after "seeing" their thoughts, they have something concrete to reflect on. These writings are also a record of a teacher's thoughts, actions, desires, joys, frustrations, questions, musings, etc. that can be critically reflected on later. This delayed reflection can give a teacher more time to consider what expressed beliefs and practices really mean and with such type of reflections, teachers can make a more in-depth and detailed analysis. The very act of writing allows teachers to step back for a moment to think about their work for a period of time that they can eventually control their own future actions. So, teaching journals can be used as a way to explore the origins and implications of a teacher's beliefs about language teaching (and learning), and as a way of documenting a teacher's classroom practices (Richards and Farrell, 2005). Teachers can then compare their stated (written) beliefs with their recorded classroom practices in order to monitor for any inconsistencies (Farrell, 2007). In this way, second language teachers can use teaching journals as both a problem-posing and problem-solving device for reflecting on teaching activities for developing new teaching ideas, with the ultimate aim of legitimizing their classroom practices. This book also reports on the regular journal entries of the three experienced teachers over the two-year reflective period (Chapter 4).

As mentioned in Chapter 1 under data analysis, the teacher reflection group reported on in this book thus used group discussions and teaching journals as their main tools for reflection. Then transcripts from these reflective modes (group discussions and journal writing) were scanned again to examine their *teaching beliefs*, and *teacher roles*, as well as important *critical incidents* that occurred in their teaching during the period of systematic reflections. I will briefly outline each one in the sections that follow.

### Teacher beliefs

Teaching is a complex activity with the teacher making many hundreds of decisions each day in each class. The behaviors that outsiders see may seem to be docile or as many think: "teachers just talking" are all fuelled by a teacher's beliefs about what they think they should be doing in their classrooms. In fact, all teachers' instructional choices in their lessons are influenced by their network of prior knowledge and beliefs and these networks are complex and usually unconsciously held. A teacher develops his or her assumptions and beliefs of teaching and learning over a career these are rarely subject to change unless they are consciously reflected on. As Richards and Lockhard (1994: 30) have pointed out, "teachers' belief systems are founded on the goals, values, and beliefs teachers hold in relation to the content and process of teaching, and their understanding of the systems in which they work and their roles within it." Indeed, even though ESL teachers may have graduated from the same teacher education programme, they more than likely conceptualize their work in different ways and over their careers, form different sets of beliefs that are based on their ideas of teaching and learning ESL. So, in order to understand how teachers approach their work it is necessary to understand the values, beliefs, and principles they operate from. Reflecting on the sources of experienced ESL teachers' beliefs can allow language educators a useful lens into how experienced teachers' personal beliefs and theories influence their perception and evaluation of their teaching. This book reports on the sources of the three experienced ESL teachers' beliefs as a lens for other teachers to reflect and examine the sources of their own beliefs, values, and assumptions of teaching and learning (see Chapter 5).

### Teacher roles

Many people in society also take on different professional roles such as those of doctors or teachers. Reflecting on teacher role identity allows language educators a useful lens into the "who" of teaching and how teachers construct and reconstruct their views of their roles as language teachers and themselves in relation to their peers and their context. Within language education, Varghese, Morgan, Johnston, and Johnson (2005: 22) have maintained that, "in order to understand language teaching and learning we need to understand teachers: the professional, cultural, political, and individual identities which they claim or which are assigned to them." Thus it is important to reflect on the various roles that teachers take on during their careers as well as the roles that are imposed on them by institutions or others so that they can make informed decisions about which roles are still relevant for their needs as they continue in their careers as teachers. However, teachers do not usually consciously reflect on these roles because many have become routine for them over the years. This book reports on the roles the teachers took on over their careers and the roles that were imposed on them (see Chapter 6).

### Critical incidents

A critical incident is any unplanned and unanticipated event that occurs during class, outside class, or during a teacher's career but is "vividly remembered" (Brookfield, 1990: 84). Incidents only really become critical when they are subject to this conscious reflection, and when language teachers formally analyze these critical incidents, they can uncover new understandings of their practice (Richards and Farrell, 2005). Incidents only really become critical when they are subject to this conscious reflection, and when language teachers formally analyze these critical incidents, they can uncover new understandings of their practice (Richards and Farrell, 2005). Basically, there are two main phases of reflecting on critical incidents: a description phase followed by an explanation phase (Tripp, 1993). In the description phase, some issue is observed and documented and is later explained by the teacher in terms of its meaning, value, or role to that particular teacher. This book reports on critical incidents the three experienced teachers over the two-year reflective period (see Chapter 7).

## Reflective questions

- Have you ever been a member of a teacher reflection group?
- What are the advantages and disadvantages of joining a teacher reflection group?
- Have you ever written regularly about your work?
- What are the advantages and disadvantages of writing about your work?
- Have you ever reflected on your teaching beliefs?
- Have you ever reflected on your teacher roles?
- Have you ever reflected on critical incidents in your classroom?

## Recognizing a reflective practitioner

Before concluding this chapter it is important to consider one remaining aspect of reflective practice that I think is important for readers to consider at this point of the book and for this I return to the ideas of John Dewey's (1933) work on reflective inquiry. Dewey noted that in order to engage in reflective practice, teachers would need to have at least three attributes of reflective individuals that remain important today: open mindedness, responsibility, and wholeheartedness. Open mindedness is a desire to listen to more than one side of an issue and to give attention to alternative views. Responsibility means careful consideration of the consequences to which an action leads; in other words, what is the impact of reflection on the learners. Wholeheartedness implies that teachers can overcome fears and uncertainties to critically evaluate their practice in order to make meaningful change. Later Dewey (1933) added a fourth attitude that needed to be cultivated in order to engage in reflective practice and that is directness. Directness implied a belief for Dewey that something is worth doing which I think nicely sums up why teachers should engage in reflective practice: because it is worth doing. The main idea of what we do is that we teach students rather than lessons.

Another interesting question concerning reflective practice and related to the attributes of a reflective practitioner is: How would you recognize a reflective practitioner if you saw one? In order to consider this we need to consider some assumptions about reflective practice. These assumptions are as follows:

1. Engaging in reflective practice involves a process of problem-posing, solving problems, and reconstructing meaning. This problem-posing and problem-solving is seen as a healthy, normal, and creative process.
2. Reflective practice is evidence-based in that teachers are actively seeking concrete evidence and knowledge about their practice. This means teachers must gather data about their practice. The results of engaging in such evidence-based reflective practice may mean an affirmation of current practices or making changes, but these changes will not be based on impulse, tradition, or the like; they will emerge as a result of analysis of concrete evidence.
3. Reflective practice is also dialogue-based rather than teachers reflecting in isolation. This assumption is very important to the contents of this book as reflective practice was carried out by the three teachers are a group rather that three individual teachers self-reflecting in isolation. As Kumaravadivelu (2012: 95) has noted: "Teaching is a reflective activity which at once shapes and is shaped by the doing of theorizing which in turn is bolstered by the collaborative process of dialogic inquiry."
4. Reflective practice in teaching is manifested as a stance toward inquiry; an attitude toward understanding classroom and teaching life. Reflective practitioners see classrooms as centers of inquiry where not only students learn but also teachers learn. Where reflective thinking is identified by a process, a reflective practitioner is identified by a stance towards reflection. In other words a reflective teacher can be observed as one who is constantly asking questions about his or her practice such as what am I trying to achieve? How am I trying to do this? What is the result? How do I know this is the result?

Do I see any need (my students' needs mostly) to change any of my approaches or practices now that I am aware of the above answers. As Oberg and Blades (1990: 179) maintain, reflective practice "lies not in the theory it allows us to develop (about practice or reflection) but the evolution of ourselves as a teacher. It's focus is life; we continually return to our place of origin, but it is not the place we left."

5. The demonstration of reflective practice is seen to exist along a continuum; people vary in opportunity, ability, or propensity to reflect. As such it may be unreasonable or even unhelpful to expect teachers consistently to engage in reflection at every moment because it could lead to too much second guessing of the experiences that a teacher has developed over a career of teaching. Most teachers engage in some sort of reflection if only just thinking about a class on the way home after a day teaching.

## Reflective questions

- What level of each of the above attributes of a reflective practitioner do you possess?
- Which attribute is most important for you and why?
- Examine and comment on your understanding of each of the five assumptions discussed above.
- Can you add more assumptions of your own about reflective practice?

## A caution

Many educators assume a positive relationship between reflective teaching and teacher effectiveness. However, education has a long but disappointing history of attempts to relate personality variables, styles, or qualities in teachers to student learning outcomes. Consequently, reflection and reflective practice has not escaped from its share of criticism. Jackson (1968) wondered pessimistically about the potential for success of efforts at developing reflective teachers. Jackson (1968: 151) says: "Even if [teacher] did possess the inclinations and skills for reflection ... they might receive greater applause from intellectuals, but it is doubtful that they would perform with greater efficiency in the classroom." However, Jackson's use of efficiency as sole criteria for evaluating the worth of reflective teaching does not address the value of reflecting for making teachers more thoughtful and more aware about what they teach even if we cannot measure their so-called effectiveness.

Indeed, some educators may say that a lack of a reflective view from some teachers may be an adaptive response and a natural consequence of the fast-paced classroom. They say that reflection and teaching are incompatible; reflection would paralyze a teacher from action and result in a dysfunctional classroom. How can teachers possibly reflect all the time and still get on with teaching their students they wonder. In addition, Goodson (1994: 30) has pointed out that the concept of teacher as researcher has some problems that are not easy to answer:

1. It frees the researchers in the university from clear responsibility from complementing and sustaining the teacher as researcher.
2. The teacher as researcher focuses mainly on practice; are we seeking to turn the teacher's practice into that of a technician which turns teaching into a routinized and trivialized delivery of predesigned packages.

Important issues about reflective practice were also raised by Hatton and Smith (1994, pp. 34–36) such as the following:

1. Is reflection limited to thought processes about action, or more bound up in the action itself?
2. Is reflection immediate and short term, or more extended and systematic? That is, what time frame is most suitable for reflective practice?
3. Is reflection problem-centered, finding solutions to real classroom problems, or not? That is, whether solving problems should be an inherent characteristic of reflection?; group discussion and journal writing are widely used as a tool for reflection but they are not problem-solving.
4. How critical does one get when reflecting? This refers to whether the one reflecting takes into account the wider political, cultural, and historic beliefs and values in finding solutions to problems.

Hatton and Smith (1995: 36) also see a number of "barriers which hinder the achievement of reflective approaches."

- Reflection is not generally associated with working as a teacher; reflection is seen as a more academic exercise.
- Teachers need time and opportunity for development.
- Exposing oneself in a group of strangers can lead to vulnerability.
- The ideology of reflection is quite different than that of traditional approaches to teacher education.

## Reflective questions

- Look at the criticisms above concerning engaging in reflective practice. Which do you agree with and consider the biggest barriers to conducting reflective practice?
- Which do you consider not an issue conducting reflective practice?
- What would the role of the university researcher then turn into if not to help teachers develop their practice?
- Is teacher as researcher deeming the practicing teacher's work?
- Can you list any other problems associated with conducting reflective practice?

## Conclusion

Reflective practice helps free the teachers from impulse and routine behavior because it allows teachers to act in a deliberate, intentional manner and avoid the "I don't know what I will do today" syndrome. Reflective practice is thus more than mulling over a particular issue; it involves systematically looking at what we do, how we do it, why we do it, what the outcomes are in terms of our student learning, and what actions we will take as a result of knowing all of this information. If English as a second or foreign language teaching is to become recognized as a professional body, then experienced teachers need to be able to explain their beliefs, values, assumptions, as well as their judgments and actions in their classrooms with reasoned argument. Can you imagine asking a medical doctor to explain why he or she is prescribing you a particular course of treatment and medication and he or she is unable to but says "it feels correct"! So too language teaching professionals must be on their guard against unexplainable thoughts and actions so that they too can be considered a serious profession. In this chapter I have suggested that when language teachers engage in evidence-based systematic reflective practice by meeting regularly in a teacher reflection group, writing about their practice, and examining their beliefs, roles, and particular critical incidents they can become more aware of who they are and where they are going. Indeed, ESL teachers, meeting regularly as outlined in this chapter, will then begin to see how much they have in common, become more comfortable explaining their teaching routines to themselves and others, and come to experience and enjoy a new level of self-articulated professionalism which will also be recognized by other professions.

# 3
# Reflection through Discussion

## Introduction

As mentioned in the previous chapter, in their mid-career years some language teachers may feel the need to take stock of their professional lives and one of the most effective ways of doing this is to engage in some form of reflection such as talk in a teacher development group. Because teaching is such an isolated act with one teacher and any number of students in a classroom (door usually closed), teachers do not readily gather together to talk about their teaching because some may feel insecure sharing their ideas after years in isolation. However, Farrell (2007) has suggested that teachers who come together to talk about their teaching can be very effective and as a result of participating in such groups, teachers can change their thinking about their work and ultimately become more confident practitioners. One reason for such effectiveness is that teacher reflection groups facilitate dialogue, sharing, and collaboration and the exchange of resources, information, and expertise while also offering "hope to others wishing to break out of the shells of isolation separating teachers from their colleagues as well as from teacher educators" (Oprandy, Golden, and Shiomi, 1999: 152). This chapter outlines and discusses in some detail what these three ESL college teachers talked about at the group meetings in an attempt to interpret these career experiences in terms of their newly emerging concern with plateauing in their mid-careers. As the group discussions turned out to be the main way the teachers reflected on their practice, many issues came up during these discussions. However, in the interests of space I only focus on three main and broad topics that they teachers spent most of their time talking about (in order of frequency) *school context, perceptions of self as teacher,* and *learners* (these accounted for over 75% of all group comments). Embedded in these discussions are also more details about the role of the administration in institutions with ESL programs. Each of these three topics are intentionally broad so as to include as much as possible without distracting readers with small and passing issues that were not of real concern. However, I also realize that I may have omitted some important topics by not including any issue that was not discussed in detail. By going through these topics and looking through these three experienced teachers' "windows of practice," and by taking the time to reflect with the reflective questions that follow each section I hope teachers, teacher educators, and administrators can find relevance to their particular context. As with all the other chapters presented in this book, the findings presented in the sections that follow can be incorporated into the teacher training and education courses so that teacher learners can become more aware of the realities of the teaching contexts they are about to enter.

## What the teachers talked about

The following sections outline in some detail the three main topics the teachers talked about during the group meetings. These three topics in order of frequency were school context, perceptions of self and their learners. Although each is presented in a separate section it will become evident that all three are intertwined and that divisions between them can become blurred at times. This shows the complexity of what ESL teachers have to consider in their daily practices as language teachers.

### School context

The most frequent topic in the group discussions was about *school context* and in particular comments focused negatively on the school administration, but positively about their interactions with other ESL teacher colleagues. For example, when they talked about their school's administration they suggested that the administration did not really know what an ESL teacher's many duties and roles were within the school, and that they sensed that there was a real disconnect between administration and the ESL teachers in the school. As a result, all three teachers agreed that they felt underappreciated by the administration. They also felt a special pressure as ESL teachers that other teachers in the institution may not have felt, that of student retention because all were well aware the institution's desire to move the international students into other programs in the institution as soon as possible after "successfully" completing their ESL courses. One administrator explained the function and role of the ESL Department in the institution as follows: "The function of the ESL team/department is primarily to make sure that we offer a strong English for Academic Purposes program, so that as many as possible of our international ESL students continue at the college in regular diploma/graduate certificate/applied degree programs." However, the three teachers said that they felt a certain amount of pressure to balance this issue of retention and providing quality lessons for their students. T2 pointed out: "I feel that that pressure is there. I mean we work in a very good place in terms of, you know trying to balance out an education and learning, learning is important. But it starts to trigger that sense of 'we've got to keep the customers happy. We've got to keep them paying their money and that kind of thing'."

Regarding the duties of ESL teachers in the school, in several group meetings the teachers expressed their doubts as to whether or not administrators in the college knew exactly what the ESL teachers really do each day. T2, for example, noted: "I don't think they know all that we do. All ESL teachers do an awful lot and differently." T1 expanded on this comment and suggested that even those colleagues outside the ESL Department may also not understand what they do; she said: "People outside of ESL, including the administration, only know what the job is superficially, but that they do not really appreciate or understand completely the work" that she and other ESL teachers do in the college; T1 continued:

> I think they know what we do superficially. Okay, you teach your class, they might know that. But beneath the surface of that statement, I don't think they appreciate in the sense of value. But I don't think they understand what that entails in terms of the preparation, the interruptions of the students, the follow up, the extra activities, and so on that we have to do in our role.

Regarding the extra activities mentioned above, all three teachers noted that the extra work these outside activities entail is not recognized or rewarded by administration. As T1 noted, the administration was "not even aware of the extra-curricular activities" and furthermore, T2 wondered if the administration "even cared about this." For example, T1 said that even though it is not part of her job description to have students over at her house, she nevertheless wanted to do it because "it is a nice thing to do." T1 continued:

> It's not the job description. Nobody asks us to do it. Nobody cares if we do it or not. We don't look at each other and say, "You didn't have students over." There is no pressure to do it. It's something that, maybe you like your students.

T2 said that she found herself in a similar position when trying to find a balance between trying to be a "good teacher" and the many different non-teaching duties that the ESL teachers must do. She noted that these should really be taken care of by administrative assistants but the administration would not allot any such assistants to the ESL department, which according to T2 was "a further indication of the administration's general [negative] attitudes toward various aspects of running a language school [the ESL Department in this case]."

In contrast to their negative dealings with the school's administration, all three teachers said that they really enjoyed collaborating with their ESL colleagues because of they suggested the isolated nature of the job of teaching. As T2 explained, "So often you are out on your island 'Oh my God! Here I am by myself. Am I the only one having this issue?'" An example of collegial interactions with colleagues was when T1 talked about working with another ESL teacher in the same institution (but outside the teacher reflection group reported on in this chapter) about her struggles teaching the same level class and she realized that as a result of her discussions with this colleague, she began to see her colleague "in a whole new role" as a "critical friend"; she said that her colleague "clicked into almost a mentor mode because she had taught speaking so much more than I have recently and then she came up with these [teaching] ideas." This critical friendship made her realize the value of colleagues collaborating; she continued: "It just started to hit me that as we were taking that we could do more together than this; that's what you need between colleagues to get this kind of thing going." T1 said that as a result she has since begun to meet with other colleagues to discuss her teaching; she said: "I'm meeting with other teachers and we're talking about our teaching. We're trying to become better teachers. I like to share what I learn with them." T3 also reflected on her collaborations with other ELS teacher colleagues within the college and how she found such collaborations reassuring for her own teaching; she noted: "It was just one of those things where you always knew but it was kind of nice to see that people have some sort of common characteristics and you have to understand how each other is both working together as a staff."

## Reflective questions

- Outline your school context: who are in the administration and how do they interact with the ESL teachers?
- Why do you think the teachers talked most about their school administration?
- Why do you think the administration does not know what an ESL teacher does? Is this also the case in your institution?
- Do you collaborate with your colleagues?
- If not, why not? If yes, how do you collaborate?

### Perception of self as teacher

The category perception of self as teacher focused on teachers' comments about their teacher roles, and insights about themselves as teachers. The first theme that emerged in this category was a real concern with how to balance their professional life and their personal life. T1, for example, wondered about how she could balance her personal and professional life: "I wonder am I putting too much in? I try to make sure that I always have lots of free time. I don't take work home at night and slave over it." She noted however that she has to be careful of letting herself fall into working more because she is aware of the negative consequences of an imbalanced work world; she noted:

> I come from a workaholic family, right? I don't think *workaholism* is something to be proud of. When I see myself going in that direction, I dislike it and that's what gets me to shift. When I notice an imbalance in my world, I hate it because I see what *workaholism* did to my family and it's not good.

T2 noted that she tends to isolate herself from others in order to get her work done, but that this does not always result in the completion of her work; she said: "I've cut myself off completely so I can get my work done and I'm still not getting my work done. But I'm torn in too many directions, trying to get my ESL classes ready. It's just all about time." T3 said that she realizes that she should not feel guilty and just complete certain tasks to a position of burnout; instead she realized that she should think about the job long term:

> If you get to the point of resentment, that's not good. I don't feel guilty when I don't do something. If I don't, I won't because I have to stay long term in the job, I can't burn myself out. I don't lay guilt on myself that way.

Another "balancing" issue for all three teachers was how they could make their lessons both fun and meaningful given a teacher's personality. T2, for example, noted the conflict she feels about how to keep her students happy while at the same time teaching them something concrete that may not be "fun"; she continued: "I think there is a big conflict between keeping people happy and helping them to learn what they need. That conflicts in my mind too." T1 noted that she even went so far as to try to change her teacher personality to make her classes "bubbly" and although she said that the response from the students was positive, she said that she found it difficult and exhausting for her to keep this "new bubbly personality" because it really was not her and it was exhausting for her; she continued:

> I thought, "just try giving a little bit more to students, pay more attention." Then it was really great. It was wonderful. The students were really happy. But I was so tired. I can't do that. I'm not bubbly all the time. I'm not social all the time.

T3 said that sometimes she wondered with how to act in front of her students in the first meeting each semester because they sometime misinterpret who she really is as a teacher and a person. Although she noted that she tells them on the first day about her expectations for the class that semester, she said: "once they see my fun personality, they sometimes misinterpret my expectations." She said that they sometimes think she is too easy and may not take her seriously, therefore, she said that she feels she must remind them every once in a while what she really expects and tells them so. Sometimes she even walks out in the middle of class if they do not take her seriously:

> I start off and I try to set the expectations on my part right at the beginning and then I always get misinterpreted, you know: "T3's fun! T3's this! T3's that!" And then inevitably my tests are too hard and they feel quite shocked. And [then] I listed all the reasons that I felt they could be responsible.

The teachers also talked about how they perceive their students' reactions during their lessons for indications of how they are learning. For example, T1 said that she is aware of how much feedback she receives about the effectiveness of her teaching by "reading the body language" of her students:

> I became aware of how much I read in the class all the time. Okay, this person has got his head down. Is he bored? Is he sleepy? Is he

whatever? That person is chatting over there. That person looks miserable. Who's paying attention? I'm trying to balance with what's happening in the classroom. I'm experiencing whether it's resistance or something new for them, so it's a struggle.

T2 also noted that she can looks at her students' reactions as an indication of whether or not they seemed to be learning from her:

It's the look on their faces and their body language. With one group of people my instinct is that they were genuinely involved in learning from each other, which I always find to be very intriguing that they can actually learn from each other. Then the other group couldn't have given a hoot about what each other had to say. It's all about, what am I going to learn today and I don't really want to listen to the rest of these people's ideas, which right away gave me a sense of those two different groups of classes who are studying exactly the same thing.

From the student responses, T2 said that she gets a sense of whether or not her lesson for a class was effective: "In the one group I was very, very happy. I left there thinking this went exactly how I had imagined it would be. I was very, very happy and they enjoyed it because they all looked happy and answered all the questions."

All three teachers also discussed the idea that quick lesson planning works for them, but this can also cause classes to be a bit boring or haphazard. They mention that it is not necessary to be very structured and that good classes can be had if they aren't totally planned or "followed to a tee." However, they also noted that planning carefully helps them feel more comfortable in the classroom.

T1, for example, noted that sometimes her classes turn out well even if it was not planned that way:

As the lesson went on I was modelling and it turned out to be useful in the end. It was unplanned. I mean partly through when I realized what I was doing, and then I started to think more actively about it. Oh this is working out well. Let's run with this one then and go with it.

T2 noted that time can be a factor when planning lessons because she has so many other duties to attend to: "I can take something off the internet and have a reading lesson in 10 minutes flat. Is it a good lesson? Probably not! It works but I'm not happy with it. That's the problem with it. It's just that balance and if that's how much time I have." But T2 also noted that she is not happy as a result of this rushed lesson planning:

> I leave the ESL classes often feeling not content with what went on, feeling that there were other things that I could have done if I just had some more time I could have done this or I could have done that and it would have been so much better. I write it down and I say, next term I am going to do that and I still don't have enough time.

The teachers also reflected on their own development (or lack of development) as teachers in a type of stock taking reflective moment. Of course, these reflections began at the establishment of the teacher-initiated reflection group when they all noted a need for some change in their professional lives. Apart from the teacher quote in the title of this paper, T1, realized that she needed to go out of her comfort zone and reflect on her development but that she was unsure of this too and hence her reason for joining the group to reflect on her work. T1 revisited her early reflections at the end of the project when she noted that she had reflected on most of her teaching life during that past semester; she remarked: "We are definitely moving out of our comfort zone there. If you want professional development as an ESL teacher, you need to revisit everything." T3 also suggested that she has grown as a teacher during the period of reflection because now instead of letting student problems get to her as she had in the past, now she does not let them bother her so much as she now realizes that learning is a student responsibility; she commented: "Now I feel like I'm sort of swaying the other way but I just keep saying to them, some of them will apologize 'I'm sorry I missed your test', and I want to say, 'I don't care. It's your learning, it's not mine'."

When discussing their perception of self as teacher, each teacher considered how they could better balance professional life and personal life with all three coming to the conclusion after a lot of discussion that it was not a good idea to let work life deeply influence their personal lives. Another "balancing" issue the teachers discussed within this topic was how they could make their lessons meaningful and interesting without changing their teacher personality. After much discussion, the teachers agreed that they could not change their personality to suit the students' interests because it was too difficult and exhausting.

### Reflective questions

- Would you consider teaching an "isolated" profession?
- If yes, why? If no, why not?

- How do you balance your life as a teacher?
- Do you ever feel guilty about not preparing your classes well?
- Is it possible to make lessons both meaningful and joyful? Why or why not?
- Do you ever change your teaching personality to meet your students' needs?
- Do you plan your lessons in detail?
- Do you ever engage in "quick planning"?
- How do you gauge your students' reactions during lessons?
- What role does your students' reactions during lessons play on your evaluation of how a lesson is going or had gone?
- What is your "comfort zone" as a teacher, and do you ever try to move out of it as a teacher?

### Learners

From an official position the majority of their learners were English for Academic Purposes (EAP) students whose aim was to be accepted for regular college programmes: as one administrator put it: "we hope as many as possible of our international ESL students continue at the college in regular diploma / graduate certificate/applied degree programs." They also teach new immigrants in small ESL programs as well as run regular summer programmes for any ESL students who may want to sign up.

Within the group discussions the category learners focused mainly on how they perceived their students' responded to their teaching and their lessons. For example, T1 told a story about a student who would look really angry when he did not understand what she was teaching him: "He's got a really, really angry face." However, she noted that she would not just give him the correct answer as this would not help him learn anything; she said: "Well he hadn't understood the part of the story and he'd missed one of the key points. I didn't want to just change his answer. I wanted to show him where to look for it, right?" However, she was frustrated then with him because she said he would not react after that and "withdrew emotionally from the lesson" and then she said he continued in this manner for the remainder of the semester and she really did not know how to deal with him, so she just let him be. She reflected: "He doesn't give me anything. He just looks at me and when it happened, from the very first day of school he was like that and at first I thought, what?"

T2 also related how she feels frustrated with her students and especially when some of them come to class late or just do not bother to try when they do come to class. T2 said: "they're coming late and they're falling asleep all day." T2 said that she blames the media for their short attention spans when there are in class; she continued: "I think they have a shorter attention span because of media and television and computers and all that kind of thing. They want constant stimulation." T1 also relayed her frustrating experience with one student who would never be prepared for class, would not work on his tasks by himself and had a very short attention span to the point where he even closed his eyes during lessons and put his head down on the desk; she said:

> He's like sleeping right? I don't even think he had a book. He always borrows my book. Anyway, I'm like [calls the student's name] "Have you finished?" And he's just stretched out there on the desk head in elbow. I'm like, "Why don't you do this?" He looks at me like, "I will. I will." I'm like, "[names student], It's my job." He's laughing and I can see the other students in the background laughing, right. They're like, "yeah, yeah." You have to keep on him because he needs someone to, a little bit to keep on him.

Similarly, T3 noted that students needed to be constantly stimulated but rather than just relay these problems she also noted that because of the discussion in the teacher reflection group the previous week on the same topic, she said that she decided to talk to her class in order to help them find some sense of excitement when learning English:

> So I put them in groups and I asked them, "How important is it to you to have enjoyment in your class?" And then what kind of things that are done in class is valued? It was sort of this even balance of "Well, if I'm not enjoying it it's boring," and I was saying, "Well wait a minute. Is the opposite of boring enjoyment or interesting?" They stopped and looked at me and went "Oh!"

Another theme that addressed the issue of relationships with the learners and what is appropriate. All three teachers suggested that when teachers can identify with their students beyond the classroom, it tends to make teaching in class easier and more effective but at the same time it also takes up a lot of their free time and energy. So, they all wondered about where they should draw a line between their professional and private lives. T3 noted that it is difficult for her to know exactly where to draw this line because she said although she "gets energy" from constant interactions with her students outside class this also results in burnout for her as she gets exhausted:

My burnout! I'm sure comes from the constant interaction but I also get energy. But just yesterday [some students] wanted to ride in my car, fine. I thought we'd just hit the Mall and they would go their way and I would go mine, but they didn't. They stayed with me and I was with them all the time [in the Mall] for a few hours.

All three teachers also wondered how much responsibility they have in nurturing, helping, and taking care of their students. For example, T2 noted that teaching ESL is similar as "being in a helping profession where you are constantly helping people. I can say, for sure, last year I had at least 5 people crying in my office for various different reasons and not because of me or anything I did." The other teachers had similar experiences about spending time with students outside of class listening to their problems; as T3 noted: "I would be the first one, to sit down and let the students talk and cry because I am implicitly a helper, that's just who I am and I just have to fix it [whatever problem the students have], because I know that get my energy from people."

That said all three teachers said that they enjoy being in the classroom and around students as the most satisfying and rewarding part of their professional lives. For example, T1 said that she enjoys being with her students and becomes calm once she enters the classroom: "I think for the most part, teachers like to be with students. That's what they do. They enjoy being with them. "Let's just get in the classroom." And people become much calmer, like "this is my class." Indeed, T2 stated that after this period of reflection she now realizes that for her being in the classroom is the center of her calling as a teacher; she said: "I find that I know that I love teaching. I know that when I hit that classroom everything that's personal, that's wrong or bad, that's not teaching, stays outside the door."

## Reflective questions

- What type of learners do you teach?
- What are some good points about them and what are some negative points about them?
- Do you ever feel frustrated with your students?
- If yes, what situations create this sense of frustration?
- What would you do if a student suddenly got angry with you?
- What would you do if a student was sleeping in your class?
- What kind of relationship do you think ESL teachers should have with their students?

- Do you think ESL teachers should have contact with students outside of their ESL classes?
- Do you think that ESL teachers have different responsibilities for their students than other content teachers?
- If yes, what are these responsibilities?

## Teachers' reflections on discussions

All three mid-career teachers entered the group discussions with the idea that they needed to do something about their own professional development. They were plateauing and although only one of the three actually said this, the other two exhibited symptoms of plateauing and the need to get a sense of renewal in their lives as ESL teachers. I believe they achieved this with the help of the group discussions. The teachers said that they regarded group discussions very highly and believe they are extremely valuable for their personal and professional lives. The main positive comments about group discussions was that they were empowering, and that it forced them to think and reflect on why they do what they do. They suggested that the group discussions encouraged them to consider best practices and as a result to seek improvements in their own teaching practices. They noted that the group discussions give them a sense of awareness of what they do in the classroom, and helped them come to the realization that they are established ESL teachers. T1 remarked that she was only interested in the content of her teaching without judgment and regardless of what she discovered because she really wanted to understand her teaching better; T1 continued: "Throughout the group discussions I wasn't concerned by the positives or the negatives or the neutrals. I mean I looked at them and it was interesting and there were not really surprising. So I feel empowered by our group discussion." On reflection T1 said that the group discussions encouraged her to look at her practices and as a result she now reflects constantly about what she does. T1 remarked: "I truly appreciate the heightened sense of awareness that has been growing within me as time goes on. I find myself stopping to think twice about the choices I make for what I do in the classroom." T3 said that she has become a more confident teacher after engaging in the group discussions over the two semesters; she noted: "These two terms of our meeting/sharing/questioning have helped to instill a more consistent habit of reflection for me." T2 said that she sometimes stops while teaching wondering about what she is doing and now that the group discussions have ended she noted that she must rely on her own decision making and as such misses the group discussions. "Now I must consider alternatives in my teaching by myself so I miss our discussions." Overall, then it seems the teachers felt that group discussions allowed them to explore what they and their colleagues do and why and thus gave them the feelings of empowerment to move ahead in their careers as ESL teacher. T2's comments at the final group discussion really sums up their collective experiences with the group discussions:

> I was really happy with our last meeting and have been thinking about it for the last few days. I went away feeling that we had found some direction and that there were some common interests that we could explore.

## Conclusion

This chapter outlined and discussed what three experienced ESL college teachers in Canada talked about in group discussions as they reflected on their work over a period of time. The three most important topics were: school context, perceptions of self as teacher, and learners. In addition the group discussions were supportive as they were held in a non-threatening environment and all three teachers used the discussions to develop a new understanding of their practice as well as gain supportive feedback from peers. Such a group of teachers working together can achieve outcomes that would not be possible for an individual teacher working alone. Of course different groups of teachers reflecting in a teacher reflection group may come up with different topics because we are not all the same nor do we all teach in the same context. Nevertheless, the three main topics covered in this chapter will resonate with most language teachers because we all work in a particular context and we have perceptions of ourselves as teachers, and of course we all have students (learners). However, we rarely consciously reflect on these nor do we openly discuss them with other colleagues. I hope the results of the group discussions outlined in this chapter provide such a forum for future groups of teachers as they begin to reflect on their practices.

# 4
# Reflection through Writing

## Introduction

Journal writing can provide teachers with a written record of various aspects of their practice such as classroom events in which they can later review and can thus assist them in gaining a deeper understanding of their work (Farrell, 2004). In addition, teaching journals can be used as a way to explore the origins and implications of a teacher's beliefs about language teaching (and learning), and as a way of documenting a teacher's classroom practices (Richards and Farrell, 2005). This chapter outlines what the three teachers wrote about during the two-year reflective period. We defined writing as a sit-down formal reflection time that could occur at any period during the reflective period and it was conducted on a computer. At the first group meeting all three teachers agreed that in general each would keep an ongoing journal account of their experiences during the period of the group's existence. They agreed at the beginning that they could write about anything, whenever they wanted, but they also agreed to write at least one entry after an "event" was experienced; an "event" was to include a class observation and/or discussion, and a group meeting. All three teachers wrote many journal entries and despite their very busy schedules had lots to write about concerning their practice. As with my recommendations presented at the beginning of the previous chapter I hope teachers can also compare the findings from the teachers' journals with their own teaching experiences.

## What the teachers wrote about

Globally, the main topics (in order of frequency) the teachers wrote about in their journals throughout the two-year period were *teaching approaches and methods, evaluating teaching,* and *perception of self as teacher.* Although these topics were similar as the teachers talked about in the group discussions, you will see they tended to use journal writing to further reflect on particular topics and issues and they found that the built-in delayed reflection that is inherent in the act of writing seemed to help them think more about these topics. Their writings also seemed to be more personal and evaluative and tended to result in more intense, deeper reflections than was the case during the group discussions. I now present these main topics in some detail and in order of their frequency of occurrence in their journals.

### Teaching approaches and methods

The category teaching approaches and methods accounted for most of the writings of all three teachers. When considering their approaches and methods, the teachers focused mainly on how they could make their students' learning experience in class more effective. For example, T1 in her first journal entry she wrote about her approach to teaching reading and how she planned her reading lessons at the beginning of each term after she had received her students input during her first lesson with them. She wrote:

> I spent most of the first class getting to know my students and had them choose the chapters of the text that interested them. This is really important to me because I know that reading can be especially challenging and boring for students when it follows the typical read and answer the comprehension question pattern, which is the design of my text.

She then wrote about what she covered in her reading classes and her reflections on what happened in her classes as well as what she perceived her students got from these classes. Sometimes she said that she was not sure what her students were thinking during her lessons and she worried about this. For example, she wrote:

> In my reading classes we finished reading our graded readers and spent two hours watching the related video. I think that most really enjoyed the video, but I wonder if there are some people in the class thinking "What a waste of time."

T1 also noted that she used such media as video before because did not want to follow the usual 'read-an-test' for comprehension format that many classes as well as textbooks followed, and so she used media in opposition to the 'testing' method for teaching her reading classes; she wrote:

> When I've used a video in the past, I've had very elaborate worksheets with vocabulary, and cloze exercises and comprehension questions—but this time no. I used video as I figured it was just to accompany the reading.

T2 also reflected on her approaches and methods of teaching of reading and how she too was concerned about keeping her students involved and interested during reading classes. In her very first journal entry she wrote about her concerns that although the students seemed interested, she nevertheless wondered what they were really thinking:

> The students had done a reading about good manners around the world and cultural verbal and nonverbal taboos. They all seemed to enjoy the pre-reading comprehension and vocabulary work. My main concern in this class now is just keeping it interesting and adapting the materials to suit their needs.

T3 focused her reflections in this category mostly on her teaching of writing. She wrote mostly and specifically about how she had adapted the 'process approach' to writing that she said she followed in all her writing classes. For example, early on in her journal she wrote how she presented her students with the process approach during the first few weeks of classes:

> This week, I was teaching my class about writing a paragraph and the process of steps I would like the students to take as they plan, write, revise and edit. I explained and modelled everything on the white board for about half an hour. Then I asked everyone to write on a given topic, following the process I had just demonstrated.

She then wrote that although she may have wanted to follow the process approach to writing, however, she also became a bit frustrated because she had noticed that her students did not in fact follow it and more than likely did not want to follow such an approach to writing. She wrote: "I get a kick out of teaching a process—the writing process in this case." Then she noticed that her students may not share her enthusiasm with this approach because they do not want to write paragraphs or drafts.

She wrote: "Students don't seem big on this. They like to get to the 'meat' as fast as possible." But she would not give up on this approach so the following week she related that she explained (and modeled) slowly again why it was important for them to follow all the writing stages within this approach. She wrote:

> This week, I was teaching my class about writing a paragraph and the process of steps I would like the students to take as they plan, write, revise and edit. I explained and modelled everything on the white board for about half an hour. Then I asked everyone to write on a given topic, following the process I had just demonstrated.

After this modeling of how she had wanted her student to write, T3 mentioned that she realized that many of the students did not follow what she had presented and so naturally she wondered why they were reluctant to follow her teaching. She wrote:

> I let everyone work for a few minutes and then circulated through the room and discovered that more than 50 per cent of the students had skipped 3 of the 4 steps and had gone directly to writing out a paragraph. I wonder what prevents them from stepping out of their 'safe zones'.

In her later journal entries as a result of her reflections on her use of the process approach to writing and her students' lack of enthusiasm for such an approach, T3 began to reconsider how she could adjust her approach; she wrote:

> Maybe if I let them use or develop a process of their own, it could help with their attitude. I could do this through individual meetings in which they tell me what they feel works for them. Then my assignments could still have marks for process, but maybe not my process.

For the remainder of the semester she wrote that she would compromise her approach with her students' reluctance to follow her teaching by giving them a choice and to adjust her instruction for the remainder of the semester to how they wanted to respond to her choices; she wrote:

> The main point for this course is that I have assigned another writing task. I have told the students they can choose whether or not to follow

the writing process I taught them. I'm going to see how their paragraphs turn out. My plan is to (a) ask each student to indicate what kind of process he/she followed for this assignment, (b) compare the marks between the first and second assignment, and (c) talk to each student to get them to think about the relationship between the process that was followed and the mark (if there is any).

## Reflection questions

* What are your main approaches to teaching the four skills (reading, writing, speaking, and listening)?
* Do you make an overall plan of your approaches and methods before meeting your students?
* Do you make a plan of your approaches and methods after meeting your students?
* Do you use prescribed textbooks or do you use your own materials?
* If you use prescribed textbooks and materials, do you supplement these, and if yes, how? If not, why not?
* What would you do if your students resisted your particular approaches and methods to teaching any of the four skills?
* Would you insist on your approach? If yes, why, if no, why not?
* T3 above has a three point plan to seek a compromise when approaching her lessons; this is (1) ask each student to indicate what kind of process he/she followed for this assignment, (2) compare the marks between the first and second assignment, and (3) talk to each student to get them to think about the relationship between the process that was followed and the mark (if there is any). What do you think about this plan? Would you change any of the points by adding or taking some out?

### Evaluating teaching

Related to how the teachers approach their lessons the next major category they wrote about in their journals was how the teachers evaluated their lessons called evaluating teaching. For example, T2's evaluating of her teaching centered on the issue of student interest in her classes as she also wrote about when planning her approaches noted in the section above. In her early journal entries she wrote how her students seemed not to be interested in her teaching:

Class seemed to drag on and some learners did not seem to care too much. Some students were clearly bored. It makes me feel a little frustrated and angry, not that he or anyone else could tell. I will keep my eye on this class and think about it tomorrow.

In her next journal entry she wrote about how she feels pressure to be perceived as entertaining in all her lessons of face a negative evaluation. She wrote:

> What is the value of the entertainment factor? What is the value of the actual learning? And how do the two go together in my classes? I know that students can find something to be not immensely entertaining, even serious or dry, but still feel challenged and learn a lot.

T2 noted that she was at odds as a teacher as her view as an ESL teacher is that the students must learn English; she wrote:

> I really wonder if the classroom tasks, topics and activities I perceive to be entertaining or enjoyable are actually enjoyable to my learners. I also wonder if the learners' enjoyment of these classroom tasks is often given too much importance. I believe that how useful they find something must also come into play. I too can gladly study a list of verb conjugations and feel pretty happy when I am done. What is the role for entertainment in the language classroom?

T2 decided that although she worried about what she would find, she decided to check her perceptions about how she evaluated her lessons more systematically to see if she was correct or not:

> What I hope to learn is that I am correct in my perceptions and that I know exactly what my given group of learners is enjoying and can tell without asking them, but what if I find out otherwise? I also wonder if the learners' enjoyment of these classroom tasks is often given too much importance.... We do midterm surveys every term and my learners have never complained about me or my teaching, but I would like more specific feedback.

Consequently, T2 conducted a survey of her classes and wrote about how she made up the survey and what the results were in her subsequent journal entries:

> Today I was able to squeeze my very unscientific survey of my reading classes' likes and dislikes in to the last 10 minutes of our class. While I

was writing the survey, I decided to keep it very simple. I listed many of the classroom activities or tasks we had done over the last three weeks. I compiled the results. I just confirmed some of my instincts such as 'you can never make everyone happy'.

T2 said that she found that researching her own students' perceptions was very beneficial because she knows now rather than wonders what they think about her classes, and that she would continue to do it in the future. She said: "Overall a very interesting and useful task. I learned a lot from the surveys. I will try this again with a few variations."

T3 wrote at the beginning of the semester about how she evaluated her early lessons on a positive note; she wrote:

> Taking a look at this week in teaching, I feel like I'm off to a fairly good start. I am teaching levels that have more content to teach. It's nice to balance content with skills/strategies.

However, later journal entries saw her evaluating lessons in a more negative manner for one of her classes:

> I do not like the energy in this class. I can't get the feedback that I'm looking for, nor can I move the students on at the pace I think is appropriate for them. I'm feeling like I don't feel like teaching them. No one student is horrible, but the class as a whole is not very cohesive.

This negative evaluation of her class led her to negatively evaluate her teaching of writing in general:

> In class, I feel like we're floating. I think this is because I had a very bad week last week, and then we went into a holiday weekend. This week, I couldn't focus on what I wanted to teach. To top it off, the students were tired from their trip and some of them are sick—not an optimum week for learning, that's for sure.

Later, T3 began to recognize that she may have been too negative in her evaluations of her teaching and realized that she had some "teachable moments" with this class:

> I had a couple of moments of silent surprise this week when I heard different students at different times saying that I have taught them

slang and they like that. I was taken aback at those comments. I actually have taught idioms as they've come to me in "teachable moments", but the students think they are slang. Anyways, the point is that I might be teaching more than I think I am.

For T1, evaluating her lessons involved asked herself if her students enjoyed her lessons, and if they were successful or not. She wrote a list of questions she uses to evaluate her lessons:

What did I teach this week? How did I do it? Why? Was it enjoyable? Was it useful? Was it "successful" or "effective"? How is that defined really? Have I over-emphasized student enjoyment at the cost of learning? Is there a happy balance there? Do I take too much responsibility for student learning?

T1 then noted that teachers generally try to answer some of these questions by mainly observing their students behavior and expressions during their classes. She wrote: "Our feedback is primarily our perception of student enjoyment. We observe their behaviour in class, facial expressions, body language etc. We try to judge if learning has taken place."

After several weeks of intensive reflections on her lessons, and although she did not survey the class herself (she used the official student evaluation forms and had an observer in her classes at various times), T1 wrote about how she positively evaluated her classes as follows:

I leave the classes feeling much better. I am amazed by how I can pull a good lesson and a good mood out of a hat when the situation demands it. In the classroom, it's all about them (the students)—not me. I like that. Although I did not survey the class, my own assessment is that the lesson was both useful and enjoyable and the observations [of the class guest she invited and asked to observe her teaching] helped to inform that impression.

## Reflection questions

- Do you think teachers generally evaluate their lessons positively or negatively?
- Do you worry about student evaluations of your lessons?
- Do you use school official student evaluation forms and if so, what do you think of these?
- How do you gauge the level of student interest during your lessons?

- What do you think of surveying your students after ever lesson? How would you go about it?
- Do you ever feel like your class is "floating" and/or "dragging"? If yes, what do you do?
- What would you do if you had students in your class that you decided did not care about learning English?
- T1 came up with the following evaluative questions about her lessons:
  - What did I teach this week?
  - How did I do it? Why?
  - Was it enjoyable?
  - Was it useful?
  - Was it "successful" or "effective"?
  - How is that defined really?
  - Have I over-emphasized student enjoyment at the cost of learning?
  - Is there a happy balance there?
  - Do I take too much responsibility for student learning?
- Use this list to evaluate your own lessons. Also can you add more evaluative questions?
- T2 asks: "What is the role for entertainment in the language classroom?" What do you think is the answer?

**Perception of self as teacher**

The final topic the teachers wrote about in their journals was their perception of self as teacher. T1 was the most active writer on this category. So I focus exclusively on her entry examples in this category. T1 wrote about her awareness of her day-to-day choices in teaching:

I have my own philosophy to teaching (however conscious or subconscious it may be) but this is reflected more concretely in my day-to-day choices, my practices, and preferences in teaching. I am not an indiscriminate user of tricks in the classroom. If you ask me why I have done something in the class—I am confident that I could articulate for you why.

She then became more reflective on her need to achieve a sense of balance in her life between her work and her personal life in her later journal entries because she said this was her biggest challenge:

I see my biggest challenge as achieving a balance in my life. I am actively involved in a lot of things outside of the classroom and I enjoy that, but I stay at work too late and I come home very tired every day. Work responsibilities can overtake personal and home life.

In another journal entry she noted her confusion about how much she should put into her duties outside the classroom and how much into her actual classroom teaching and her perceived conflict between the two:

> In the last three days in addition to the "usual" classroom stuff, my tasks ranged from kitchen duties to handling student conflict to discussing changes in college policy. Do my students realize that the reason I am rushing in two minutes late is because another student grabbed me in the hall with his or her "issues."

She then wrote that she wondered if her professional life was in fact healthy and now at this mid-career stage, she wondered if she would be a teacher like this for the following years:

> Is the pace at which I'm working a healthy and normal pace? Is it healthy to be so invested in your work? What are my strengths and weaknesses as a teacher at this stage of my career? What's next? Am I really going to love doing this for another 20 years?

Her next few journal entries revealed the extent of her sense of exhaustion in her attempts to balance her duties as an ESL teacher and her personal life. For example, she wrote about her exhaustion in one entry:

> Sunday: Tired all day, why? No preparation for the week, dishes in the sink, laundry piling up, papers, papers everywhere! Feeling of chaos and frustration. Am I so exhausted at the end of the week that I can't have a normal, fun weekend?

She then wrote that although she was not feeling good after that for a few days, but that teaching made her feel better because she liked being in the classroom. She wrote:

> Tuesday: I feel I have not established a balance or pace of work that is healthy for me at this time. 12:30 Time for Class. I leave the class feeling much better. In the classroom, it's all about them (the students) not me. I like that. It's a break.

Then towards the end of the semester as T1 started to take more control of her professional and balance her work and personal life better, she noticed how writing in her journal has allowed her to see the trend of her exhaustion and frustrations trying to do everything:

> As I analyze my [journal] notes from this week first, I can see the trend already. I do not feel tired as I write this journal (as I usually do). I don't feel overwhelmed by the approaching term. I don't feel worried about what students think about my teaching. My personal issues seem less monumental. Suddenly, I feel calm and in control.

Indeed after we had finished the whole process of reflecting over a two-year period, T1 said that she had reread her journals and noted just how the topic of her health had dominated her journal writing:

> But most of all, re-reading the journal has allowed me to see once again the trend in my professional "mood/health"—the real issue for me. At one point, I noted a pattern in my journals: I was saying how tired I was every week. I knew that, but seeing it in the journal weekly really hit the point home. Re-reading these journals today as a collection shows a lot more: fatigue, emotional upset, some health problems.

## Reflective questions

- What is your philosophy of teaching?
- Is your philosophy of teaching reflected in your day-to-day practices as an educator? If yes, how are they reflected (give some examples)?
- Do you think ESL teachers have a problem balancing their professional and private lives?
- How do you balance your professional life and your personal life?
- Do you ever feel exhausted after teaching? If yes, how to you deal with this?
- Do you ever have similar experiences as T1 when she wrote: "Tired all day, why? No preparation for the week, dishes in the sink, laundry piling up, papers, papers everywhere!" How do you deal with them?
- Do you think writing a journal helped T1 to be better able to cope with her feelings of being overwhelmed? If yes, how so?
- T1 noted that seeing in her journal weekly that she was exhausted "really hit the point home." How would writing in a journal help a teacher reflect in such a way?

## The act of writing

The very act of writing seemed to produce different reflections than was the case for the group discussions. It seems the built-in mechanism inherent in the very act of writing where a teacher must stop to think about not only what he or she will write about, how he or she will write it but also what particular words he or she will actually use to articulate it. In talk we can hedge, stop, start, change in mid-sentence and even contradict ourselves. In writing all these are more difficult to do and as such we tend to be more careful with what we write. In other words the act of writing slows down our thinking so that we are in more control than when we are speaking. T1 also noted the very act of writing forced her to slow her thinking process and consider what to write. T1 noted this and other important roles for her when she was writing as follows:

> I felt that the journal had many roles: (1) it forced me to slow down, observe and reflect. I think this role should not be underestimated; teachers are busy. (2) It allowed me to unpack any emotional baggage be it personal or professional and get beyond it. (3) It identified some topics that could be discussed or explored by other means later. (4) It was an opportunity to reflect upon or synthesize points that came up from classroom observations.

T1 noted that regular writing in her teaching journal during the period of reflection provided her with the mental space for her to reflect and the more she wrote about, the more she wanted to look more deeply not only into her teaching, but also into herself; she noted:

> The journal was both a private and a public space. It gave me an uninterrupted, private space where I could explore what was important to me, although ultimately I knew it would be read by others. I could take my time with it. I was forced to identify and select topics in my own work week that I felt I wanted to investigate more. It prevented the week from flying by completely unexamined. Sometimes these were critical incidents but other times it was just general observations.

T2 also said the journal was a useful reflective experience because the act of writing helped her to focus her thoughts. T2 observed:

> I think the journal writing was useful and satisfying. I learned to think things through more carefully because I needed to express the events,

or my reactions to them, as accurately as possible and often in some detail. I found the writing of journals time consuming but very useful in allowing me to reflect in a more organized fashion. I am usually someone whose thoughts are scattered and all over the place.

T2 also noted that the act of writing made her focus on one point or issue at a time and continue with that point or issue until it was fully explored and reflected on but that she found such reflections while talking very difficult to accomplish. She observed: "In conversation I have a tendency to jump around and change the subject frequently. In writing I feel forced to follow and idea through to its end more than in speaking. I felt it focused me."

T3 also revealed that writing in a teaching journal "helped me to slow down a bit to think – something I'm not good at doing." This again seems to have been a very important function of journal writing for all three teachers. T3 also suggested that writing in a teaching journal for her was a useful place for her to sort out her ideas about her teaching approaches and that the act of writing allowed her to describe what was actually happening in a safe and clear manner. She noted that writing

[h]elped me to answer/describe what was going on in my classes in the "safest" way. By sharing my journal entries with my group members for reflection, it indirectly allowed the people in my group "into my classroom" without everyone physically being there. This was a very useful activity for us all to be able to reflect on our teaching.

That said, writing in a journal may not be for all people, never mind ESL teachers. Indeed, in the post-reflection interview, T1 noted that although she had used a diary before, initially she was not looking forward to writing regularly about her teaching. However, she later noted that she began to enjoy the experience of writing to the point where she would make sure even if she was busy, to make time to write regularly regardless. T1 noted:

Regular weekly journaling has never been a favourite thing to do, so I was not too sure how I would fare on this. As it turned out, despite initial challenges of time, I found that I thoroughly enjoyed the journal and consequently found the time to do it. I believe I even commented once that I preferred to write my journal rather than do marking or other pressing tasks. This has been a stressful time for me so I think I needed the journal.

T3 also noted that in the very beginning of the reflection process, she too was skeptical about the whole idea of writing in a teaching journal as a means of reflection because she was not used to writing. But after a few weeks (and like the other teachers) she too began to enjoy the experience of writing and the journal writing process. T3 discovered that the reason she began to enjoy writing was that before she always wrote to herself but now in this group she was writing for an audience. T3 noted:

> I was surprised that I was able to keep a positive attitude towards journaling. As I stated at the beginning of this process, I don't really enjoy/value it because I can't get motivated to write when the audience is me. As long as I was able to keep my group members in mind, I was better able to write.

## Reflective questions

- Do you like to write about your practice or even your daily life? Why or why not?
- Why would some teachers not want to write about their practices?
- An important issue associated with writing a teaching journal is that writing takes time and teachers must be motivated to find the time to write. How do you think teachers should approach journal writing given they have limited time to write?
- T1 wrote about the many roles that journal writing has for her as follows: (1) it forced me to slow down, observe and reflect. I think this role should not be underestimated; teachers are busy. (2) It allowed me to unpack any emotional baggage be it personal or professional and get beyond it. (3) It identified some topics that could be discussed or explored by other means later. (4) It was an opportunity to reflect upon or synthesize points that came up from classroom observations.

  Comment on each of these roles. Can you add more roles?

- Should teachers focus on a specific problem in their teaching and write about that or should they are going to write generally about their teaching and then look for patterns in their journal entries over time?
- Should teachers share their journals with other teachers in a group (as was the case in this example) or keep them private?

- T1 decided to omit some of the entries she did not want the other participants to read, thus continuing her writing, rather than stopping altogether in fear of revealing her reflections. What do you think of her approach?
- What do you think of on-line teaching journals and "blogs" as a way teachers can share their writing?

## Teachers' reflections on writing

As noted above, all three teachers felt that though journaling takes a lot of time out of their busy lives, is sometimes hard to do because of lack of focus and time, and needs to be thoughtfully written to make it worthwhile, writing was very beneficial and helped them reflect on their routines and practices. The fact that they committed themselves to write regularly in a journal about their practices forced them to consider what they were going to write about and hence what they were going to reflect on and why. This was much different than the group discussions outlined in the previous chapter where the teachers just came and talked about their practice without any careful consideration about what they were going to talk about. As T2 remarked:

> I was thinking all day on Sunday and Monday and then I was thinking so much that I had to write because if I didn't write it down quick, it was going to run away but not as a chore but because I didn't want to forget what I was thinking about. And I wanted to share it.

T1 agreed that "It's not a chore. It's something that I really want to do. I just have to find the moment." T2 agreed that time was the greatest issue with journal writing: "It's just finding a little bit of time in there to actually sit down and do it." T3 noted that writing make her really think about what she was doing in the classroom and how her learners were reacting to her lessons; she noted: "I found writing helped me to really think about what I do in the classroom. I watched them more and took mental notes of their body language and facial expressions. I guess it just heightened my awareness of them." In addition all of the teachers felt journaling was beneficial because it gave them an outlet to vent their frustrations, pour out their emotions, focus on specific problems or issues they're struggling with, reflect on their lives, careers, and level of burnout, and share all these things with their colleagues. T1 noted this: "I can notice it in my journals. At the beginning you've got to unpack whatever is going on, unpack the emotion." Also, they noted that writing by stream of consciousness allowed them to write down every thought and then think about it and analyze it after. Finally, all the teachers enjoyed reading others' journals and wanted others to read their journals and then discuss them. In short, the teachers felt that the journal experience was very beneficial and that it was a great source of reflection and professional development.

## Conclusion

Language teachers can write regularly about their teaching practices and then review and reflect on any observed patterns that may emerge from their writing. The act of writing forces teachers to slow down and delay reflections after they have considered what they have written. The very process of writing also teacher to organize their thoughts better and helps teachers to consciously explore and analyze their practice in a more organized fashion. Writing has its problems for teachers of course such as the time it takes to write and the fact that teachers must stop what they are doing to engage in the act of writing as noted by all three teachers in focus. However, all three teachers seemed to use writing a bit differently than the group discussions. For writing they seemed to focus more on their teaching approaches and activities than for the group discussions where they focused more generally on their school context. Perhaps this isolated act of writing can allow teachers more time to focus on teaching methods and group talk is more social and as such the working context in general would be more in focus. The chapter suggests that writing seems to be an effective means of facilitating reflection, and it has an added advantage in that it can be done alone or it can be shared with other teachers; however, if teachers share their reflection, they can attain different perspectives about their work as the results of this chapter have indicated.

# 5
# Reflection on Teachers' Beliefs

## Introduction

Teacher beliefs build up gradually over a teacher's career and are said to come from a variety of sources. Richards and Lockhart (1994) for example, have suggested that ESL teachers' beliefs can originate from any of the following six possible sources: (1) teachers' past experience as language learners. For example, if a teacher has learned a second language successfully and comfortably by memorizing vocabulary lists, then there is a good change that the same teacher will have his or her students memorize vocabulary lists too. (2) Experience of what works best in their classes. Richards and Lockhart (1994) suggest that this may in fact be the main source of beliefs about teaching for many second language teachers and as such many practicing teachers may not want to break an established, and perceived successful, routine. (3) Established practice within a school that is difficult to change because the school has always used this method. (4) Personality factors of teachers can be an important source of beliefs as some teachers really enjoy conducting role-play or group work in their classes while others are more comfortable conducting traditional teacher-fronted lessons. (5) Educationally based or research-based principles can also be a source of teachers' beliefs in that a teacher may draw on his or her understanding of research in second language reading to support use of predicting style exercises in reading classes. (6) Method-based sources of beliefs suggest that teachers support and implement a particular method in their classes, as for example, when a teacher decides to use total physical response (TPR) to teach beginning second language learners, he or she is following a method of suspending early production of language for the learner exploring the sources of teacher beliefs is an important area for reflection because reflection leads to more awareness of sources of core beliefs and that his is a necessary starting point in all teacher reflections because teachers cannot really fully develop unless they are aware of what they believe about teaching and learning and how this is translated or not into what they actually do in a classroom. This chapter explores the sources of three experienced ESL teachers' beliefs as revealed after scanning the group discussions and journal writing in terms of the key influences on their teaching style. Saracho (2000: 300) says that a teacher's teaching style reflects the "the specifics of their preparation, their instructional situation" and how "individual teachers respond to their students in their own unique way." Teaching style thus reflects the teacher's values, beliefs, and cognitive style which are reflected in how a teacher acts during the teaching and learning process in a classroom. The chapter suggests that language teachers should not only reflect on the sources of their beliefs, and teaching style, articulate these to themselves and others but also reflect on the validity of their beliefs and if they remain valid after such an exploration.

## Key influences on teaching styles

The main sources in order of frequency were *teachers' personality, teaching methods, established practice, experience of what works best,* and *experience as language teachers.*

### Teachers' personality

Just as presumed by Bailey et al. (1996) and Richards and Lockhart (1994) that language teachers may have a personal preference for a particular teaching style because it complements their teaching personality, so too did all three teachers in this group show a similar influence of their personality on their teaching styles. Teacher personality included any reference to a specific characteristic, a preference, an interest, or unique way of doing something as a teacher. For instance, T3 suggested that many of her teaching practices are influenced around her belief that storytelling is part of her personality as a teacher. In several group meetings T3 recounted how she uses stories from the very first class with any new group of students to try to lower their anxiety levels but that she never realized this until she just told the group. T3 continued:

> I never realized this before but when I come in on those first days, the students are always a little shell-shocked and worried and nervous. I just can't contain myself; I say "Hi," very bubbly, that's just my

nature. My big thing is to model somehow and telling a story is how I do it.

After T3 articulated this belief to the group, she then began to wonder if this belief was still valid, where it came from, and if she was "doing too much story telling" in her classes. For example, in the following group meeting she wondered about her teaching personality and its impact on her students' learning styles and that she did not (until now) take their different learning styles into account when she was teaching; as she remarked: "I just feel that I want to, should be, sensitive to all the learning styles in the classroom." However, after further reflection she said that she would continue to use storytelling as a main method not only because it suits her personality but also "to show my students how English really in that classroom goes into real life."

And so T3 began a period of deep reflection on how and why she used stories and expressed these reflections in later group meetings. For example, she recounted that she used storytelling when teaching grammar, which she now realizes may seem strange to others. For example, she first began to wonder if she overused stories when teaching grammar; she commented:

I was worried that there was so much information going in [to the story] that they really weren't getting my point. They may be thinking: "Why is she telling this story?" or "Oh God, here we go again," and "What does this have to do with anything anyway? I just need to get through this grammar textbook for my mark," that kind of thing.

Then she reflected more and realized that telling stories for her was a very important method for teaching grammar; T3 said, "I love telling stories, to emphasize a point of grammar." She then related a specific example of how she used storytelling in a grammar class during that previous week and called this a "Kodak moment with perfect tenses." T3 continued: "So I'll be talking away with my story and then I'll stop and say 'Present-Perfect moment' and then I'll shove in my grammar. It's fun and they seem to appreciate it."

Thus, after a process of first reflecting on her teaching personality and her teaching methods and specifically articulating her beliefs to herself and her group members that storytelling really suits her personality as a teacher, she continued to believe that storytelling as a teaching method can help her students. One student said that she was an "entertainer" and T3 took this as a compliment; however, this teacher metaphor generated a lot of group discussion in later meetings about as T2 mentioned, how much of themselves they said they "would give while teaching." T2 said that she did not like the teacher metaphor of "entertainer" as it was not in her personality and that she is not always willing to "entertain" the students. T2 said:

> I think about this whole issue of entertaining and the underlying personality contest, and all about teacher popularity. What is it that drives us all to entertain at the same time? I wonder. I don't always entertain. There are certainly days where like I say, "There's no entertaining today so just open your books".

T1 agreed with T2 about the teacher metaphor "entertainer" as she said that same week she was feeling uneasy about being "funny" in class because this also was not her personality; T2 remarked:

> I think I've been really funny this week. I can do it but then I'm tired afterward because I'm more introspective. Then I was just trying to give a little bit more to students. The students were like really happy, but I was so tired.

T1 said that many times she fakes being funny and noted that she cannot keep it up all the time in class because it was not her real personality as a teacher. T1 reflected: "I can't do that. I'm not bubbly all the time. I'm not social all the time. I have to find my own time that I relate to my students, some kind of balance between." When she reflected on the finding of a balance between her personality needs as a teacher and her perceptions of her students' needs, she realized that she would always have to be herself as a teacher regardless; T1 noted:

> When I'm more myself I have to trust that whatever is going to happen is going to happen in the class. I'm not over-prepared and I just go with what, you know the lesson is there but it's more natural. I prefer that, to just trust in the process.

## Reflection questions

- How do you think your personality influences how you teach?
- What do you think of T3's use of telling stories in her classes as a factor of her personality? Do you tell stories?

- Are you aware of your students' learning styles and if so, how to you suit your teaching personality to their styles?
- Do you take on a "teacher personality persona" that may be different that your real personality?
- Do you "fake" a teaching personality such a trying to be fully like T1?
- Should ESL teachers be themselves while teaching?
- What does T1 mean when she says: "just trust the process" in the last quote above?
- In the follow-up interviews T2 noted the link between her teaching personality and her chosen teaching methods; she remarked: "It's a given that my own personality plays an important role in what I do in the classroom. I will choose certain techniques over others most of the time just because I prefer them and because they suit my personality." What do you think?
- T1 also suggested that that "personality factors of teachers can be an important" but that she said in her follow-up interview that she was not sure how much and that she "would have to analyze my lessons over a long period of time for the trends" to see what these would be exactly. What are your views on T1's opinion?

### Teaching methods

*Teaching methods* was the next core belief source and this can refer to an established method or approach of teaching or an approach or method that the teacher used or is going to use possibly in an effort to solve a problem or find a better way of doing something. A typical example from this category of beliefs was a discussion centered on their method and approaches in their writing classes and especially all three teachers' preference for the use of process writing. However, they all noted that some students were resisting this approach and so they had to try to convince them of its usefulness as an approach to develop their second language writing. For example, T1 said that she wondered why some students did not like to collaborate when they write in her classes; she noted: "Why wouldn't the students do the process writing? Why didn't they like to share and collaborate with each other? Is it resistance or something new for them? So it's a struggle." To which T2 replied that they "must 'sell' this approach to their students"; she continued: "It's like I'm selling you process writing. Come on, buy into it."

T3 then outlined how she got her students to try to follow this method and how she was frustrated that her students did not really do what she asked; she said: "It got to the point this week where I wanted them to hand things in, so I said: 'You are going to hand in your brainstorming, outline, and your paragraphs." However, over half of her students did not hand in the brainstorming or their outlines. T3 noted:

> I set it for yesterday and what did I get? Fifty percent of the class just brought me the paragraph. Two people didn't hand anything in. And then the rest, it was just a total mish-mash and I thought, here's where you go back to "What did I say? How did they perceive it? How did it get to this?" Oh my goodness!

T2 then remarked that she had had similar frustrations when trying to get her students to brainstorm (or as she noted, "an open rebellion against the brainstorm") and do outlines; she said:

> I had exactly the same experience in my Writing class. I just spent 2 weeks on this and where is the outline? Where is the brainstorm? What did I not say? It's on a piece of paper. There is a written instruction, so you wonder.

T1 then noted that she thinks her students do not see any need for brainstorming or outlines and that maybe they should consider if they really need to do these while writing. T1 said: "They don't perceive a need for it. If I can do my paragraph without doing process writing, why do I have to do it? Do I really need to do that?" T2 then noted that the students may be doing what they want anyway; she said: "How many times do they just secretly skip to the paragraph?"

The discussion then moved to a position where the three teachers began wondering if and how they could modify their approaches and methods concerning their use of a process approach to teaching writing. For example, T2 noted that although her students should be allowed to question her approaches, they should also follow them: "You are allowed to question it but there has to be brainstorming or it [process approach] just won't work."

Then all three teachers then began to reevaluate their approach and question how rigidly they should follow the process methods in their writing classes. T3, for example, noted that one of her students usually "jumps to the paragraph and that he does have a great sense of ordering of ideas." T2 also noted that she may have to rethink bringing her students through particular steps within the process approach because writing is not always liner; T2 said:

> Process writing isn't actually linear but in the classroom we try to confine them to these linear steps, is part of the problem. Some

people like to just write stuff down and then go back and outline from there or brainstorm from what they wrote.

T2 then realized she may need to modify her approach: "So if we confine them to these steps they're not likely be able to follow." To which T1 suggested that: "it's good to be flexible in some ways" when using this approach.

## Reflection questions

- Have you ever experienced any resistance to any particular approach or teaching method you tried when teaching any of the skills of reading, writing, speaking, or listening?
- What would you have done if you asked your students to hand in various drafts of their writing and over half of them did not as T3 experienced above?
- Why do you think some students in all three teachers classes resisted "brainstorming" as a way of developing their ideas in writing?
- Do you try to "sell" your particular approach/method to teaching the various skills if your students resist?
- Have you ever modified your approaches and methods to suit your students and if so, do you consider this the same as modifying your beliefs or do you still keep the same beliefs about a particular approach?
- If you modify your approach yet keep the same beliefs as before, do you think your classes are real for you as a teacher?
- T2 says that she allows her students to question her approaches but then insists that they have to follow particular steps within an approach regardless. Do you think there is any contradiction here? Do you agree with her stance?

### Established practice

The next core belief source was *established practice* and this was basically any statement that referred to an established way of doing something or when describing a constant in their teaching. An example from established practices arose in the group meetings centered on their established practices of giving feedback. For example, T3 talked about her problem she had with one student when she gave her negative feedback on her assignment and how that student responded. T3 said: "I had a minor issue yesterday with a girl crying and then hyperventilating over my feedback." T3 was not happy with the student's reaction because she said all her students know from her established past practices what kind of feedback they will get if they do not meet her standards. T3 noted: "I think it is our responsibility to set very clear standards. You can't just be nice. This, this girl, in particular, she knows that this assignment she did is way out of her mark." T3 also noted that the student did not prepare properly for the assignment and that she should have known this because it was not the first of this type of assignment she had given the class. As T3 noted:

> What does she do the day she gets the article [to read]? Does she read it? No, she sits and drinks with her homestay mom. She comes to her appointment with me unprepared and saying "I'm very, very nervous about speaking in front of my classmates," and I said, "You have to go home and you have to prepare a lot." I'm doing her any favors. She's got to do at least another type of presentation for me and how many more in Level 5, right?

T3 then said that she reminded the student about her methods of evaluation and that these were given to all students on the first day of class: "So I said to her, 'It is very clearly laid out on the evaluation form,' which she has had since day one." Then T3 told the group how she tried to help the student to improve: "I handed her the paper with my comments and said, 'You read this and come back and talk to me because I want to give you strategies to improve'. You mentor them."

Then the other two teachers suggested that T3 may be reacting too sensitively to one student because it will be too difficult emotionally; T2, for example, said: "This kind of sensitivity ultimately going to be to your detriment because you are not going to be able to survive. There are always a few students who say, 'I'm bored and your class is this'." T1 agreed and said that she had "cultivated a thick-skin." To which T2 advised T3 that she doesn't "have to take it to heart" every time a student does not like her feedback.

The discussion then moved to the type of feedback they get from their students and how they handle this. T1 said that she listens to some of their feedback, but not all of it. T1 said:

> There is some feedback that I pay attention to and some that I don't. I got feedback on something the other day and I was like, thank you very much and I thought but I don't really care about that feedback.

T2 suggested that when she gets negative feedback from her students she also usually does not react too much. She then related a recent example of negative feedback she got from one of her students and that she did not react; she said:

> What I did was just fine. But I didn't react. I said, "Thank you very much. That's very interesting. I'm going to think about it." That's how I handled my feedback. I realized my role and his role at the time and I took that feedback for what it was meant to be.

## Reflection questions

- What are your established practices that you think influence your beliefs about teaching and learning?
- What role does the way a teacher has always done something in classes play when teaching students with diverse backgrounds?
- Do you think teachers should stick to their established ways of teaching even if these established ways conflict with their students preferred learning styles?
- How far would you go to keep an established practice if the administration said it was in conflict with their approach to teaching English?
- Do you have an established way of giving feedback to your students?
- What would you do if a student reacted emotionally to your feedback?
- Do you think T3 was overreacting herself to her student's reaction?

### What works best

*Experience of what works best*, the next source of influence on their beliefs, refers to any practice that they perceived as being successful in their work. One clear example discussed about this source of teacher belief was T1's belief about how she changed the seating arrangements in her class one day to make her students more responsive, because this had worked for her in the past. T1 noted that when she walked into her reading class that day and asked how the students were, and she said that "nobody answered." Then she said that she "looked at them and thought, a couple of them are sleepy-type, And then I decided to do an activity about 'The Bachelor' on TV. They wanted to that reading." Next, T1 decided to do a speaking activity for pre-reading activity and change the seating arrangements; T1 said:

> What I did was a speaking activity as the pre-reading. I had them, instead of being all spread out around the classroom because they

tend to me very far from me and very far from each other, I brought them together. So we did that to start it off and it was unbelievable. I really was like, Wow, I've never seen that work so well before.

T1 was so impressed with the impact of changing the seating arrangements in her reading class that she decided to change the seating again in a different way in her conversation class; she said:

> We have tables kind of like in rows, large tables. And they all sort of sit like one at a table. They are very spread out. So for this activity I had them seated along one long table and we did a conversation wheel where you talk to one person about one of the questions. Then the group switches and then you get a new partner and a new topic and you talk about it for three minutes or whatever. Then you get a new partner and new topic and keep going.

T1 noted that the class dynamics changed again with the change in seating arrangements and that the students now "had to talk to almost everybody in the class about a different topic." This was very surprising for her because she said that "they were so engaged in that. I'd never seen them like that before ever." Then T1 decided to change her next classes' seating arrangements as well as the changes seemed to be working very well and that the room she was about to teach in had caused her problems with getting her students to interact with each other in the past because of its shape; she noted in her previous classes she is: "way at the front and they're just all spread out all along the long room." T1 prepared before her class; she said, "So I went early and I changed the desks to like a square, not even a long rectangle, but a complete square so they're all facing each other again and they're all facing towards the center." T1 was so impressed with the change in her seating arrangements as she noted that it made a significant difference in how her classes interacted; she said:

> It really, really helped. I was like, "Oh, my goodness. We might be having somewhat of a breakthrough." They are actually engaged. They're staring right at each other. Maybe we can make some progress. I'll just keep it like that from now on.

## Reflection questions

- How do you determine if a method "works" in your class?
- Do you think that students' reactions are always a good indication of their learning?

- What if you are using a practice that has always worked best in your classes before but involves hard work from your students and they react negatively to this practice. Would you change your practice or would you insist on using it because it has worked well in the past?
- Do you have any method such as changing the seating arrangements that has work in the past for you that you use in many, if not all, of your classes?
- Do you think that teachers can get stuck on their beliefs about what has worked best in the past and ignore their current students' needs that may necessitate changing a particular practice to suit their learning?

### Experience as language teachers

*Experience as language teachers*, the final source of the teachers' beliefs, refers to something the teacher has learned over their careers as a language teacher. An example of this occurred when the teachers talked about how they have to use their experience as teachers to try to perceive the success of their lessons in terms of levels of student enjoyment. For example, T1 said: "Okay, this person has got his head down. Is he bored? Is he sleepy? Is he whatever, you know? That's person is chatting over there. That person looks miserable. Who's paying attention?" They then noted that they have to constantly be aware of how their lessons are going and what they need to do to keep the momentum going in their lessons and all these decisions based on their vast teaching experiences. For instance, T2 pointed out that what she has realize that her past experiences teaching in Japan where she was considered an entertainer so that she could maintain student enrollment in a language school, and thus her job is still an influential source of her beliefs about teaching. She noted how she now has to balance her teaching beliefs with the pressure of student retention in her present context as an ESL teacher; T2 remarked: "I feel that that pressure is there. I feel more so now than when we first started there that the pressure on [student] retention. We've got to keep them paying their money and that kind of thing."

Given this group discussion of the conflict of what students think they need and what teachers think they need based on their experience, T2 said that when she asked her students about what they wanted, they said that they did not like to do homework but that she "knew that they needed it" based on her experience as a language teacher. She then continued to note that many students want different things but that she "cannot provide them with everything they think they want; only what they need." That said, she decided to share her beliefs with her students. T2 remarked:

> Everybody wants something completely different. I like to present that back to them and then they get the sense that, oh you mean everybody in the class doesn't like what I like. It usually helps them to be a little bit open-minded and then we can talk about it even as a class.

After sharing her beliefs, she then noted that this sharing "makes them much more involved in the process. They feel like someone actually cares what they want." T3 noted that in her experience it is always best to talk to the students about their perceptions about how a class is going and then she related to the group about how she recently discussed this and especially the idea of "if I'm not enjoying it it's boring, right." When some students agreed with this idea, T3 said that she told them: "Well wait a minute. Is the opposite of boring enjoyment or interesting? They went Oh!" Then they all discussed different aspect of her teaching and the class and T3 explained her beliefs to them. These discussions, as T3 suggested, were very useful because they "really opened each other's eyes."

## Reflection questions

- How influential is a teacher's past teaching experiences on their current practices?
- Do you think many experienced teachers consciously reflect on these experiences?
- How important is it for a teacher to reflect on their past teaching experiences?
- Do you think that because a teacher is experienced, he or she is a "good" teacher?
- Do you think teachers should discuss their past experiences as teachers with their students?
- Bailey et al. (1996) point out that any prior belief or experience will only influence a teacher's instructional behaviors to the extent that he or she permits. What are your views on this?
- Do you think an experienced teacher shapes his or her teaching methodology to suit his or her personality rather than take notice of findings in TESOL research such as those generated from SLA studies, motivation research, reading research, and so on?

- Have your eyes ever been opened as a result of a realization of a belief, value, or assumption you had about teaching and learning a second language that may be in conflict with what you are actually doing in your classroom? If yes, how did you react?

## Role of teacher personality

It seems that all three teachers' personality has had a direct influence on how they perceive they carry out their classroom practices. Indeed, in the follow-up interviews, when I pointed out this finding to the teachers, T3 again affirmed the strong influence of her personality on her teaching methods as she said: "I know from what many students have told me that my personality definitely plays a role in how I teach. I prefer an active class, and I choose methods and activities that reflect this like role-play and group work regularly." In these follow-up interviews T2 also noted the link between her teaching personality and her chosen teaching methods; she remarked: "It's a given that my own personality plays an important role in what I do in the classroom. I will choose certain techniques over others most of the time just because I prefer them and because they suit my personality."

Given that a teacher's teaching style involves the implementation of that teacher's philosophy about teaching, it is important then for teachers to not only to become aware of their teaching styles but also what influences these so that they can reflect on their relevancy for their current practice. Indeed, an important question for ELT educators is to what extent an experienced teacher shapes his or her teaching methodology to suit his or her personality. As such, teachers should reflect on whose needs there are fulfilling when they are teaching: their own by choosing methods that suit their personality only, or their students' learning needs, and styles. Perhaps a happy medium is to try to attend to both sets of needs as all three teachers attempted in the case reported on in this chapter. However, in order to be able to achieve such balance experienced teachers will need to be given opportunities to reflect on the sources of their teaching styles and their impact on instructional decisions. In such a way, teachers will be able to make more informed decisions about the methods they choose and if these methods are still providing optimum opportunities for their students to learn.

Research in the area of teaching style also has implications for instructors in teacher education programs and for educators providing professional development opportunities for language teachers, as it has the potential to help them gain a better understanding of the different needs of language teachers with different preferred teaching styles. For example, in-service courses and continuing professional development programs could be designed to promote the more effective use of teaching styles and thus enable language teachers to use a wider variety of styles that enable them to facilitate a wider variety of diverse learning styles. In addition, given the diversity of teaching contexts, teachers, and teacher education programs need to consider which teaching styles are best suited to the diverse needs of second language learners both today and in the future.

## Conclusion

It is important for teachers to not only articulate their beliefs about their practice but also the sources of these beliefs so that they can become aware of and reflect on their usefulness to their overall goal of providing opportunities for their students to learn. Teachers should become aware of whose needs there are fulfilling when they are teaching: are they satisfying their own teaching needs by choosing methods that suit their personality, or are they attending to the learning needs of their students. Perhaps a happy medium is to try to attend to both sets of needs as was the case reported on in this chapter. As the details reported on in this chapter suggest, the main source of the three teachers teaching methods was their teaching personality and after reflecting on this, they can then consider if these chosen teaching methods really meet their students learning needs. Of course, language teachers should be encouraged to explore the sources of their beliefs and through reflection and dialogue with the self or other teachers, either affirm their current beliefs or modify them towards the reality of their teaching contexts and classrooms. When teachers are encouraged to articulate their beliefs and systematically "look" at their practice, they can become more confident practitioners, be more flexible about tolerating ambiguity and become more skillful in communicating to colleagues, teacher educators, administrators and even students about important issues related to their work.

# 6
# Reflection on Teachers' Roles

## Introduction

Over their careers, teachers tacitly construct and reconstruct a conceptual sense of who they are (their self-image) and what they do (their professional role identity). Teacher role identity includes teacher beliefs, values, and emotions about many aspects of teaching and being a teacher. Role identity is about how people come to understand themselves, not only in terms of what labels that may have been bestowed or have had thrust on them such as "wonderful," "smart," but also as Urrieta (2007: 107) has suggested, how they "come to 'figure' who they are, through the 'worlds' that they participate in and how they relate to others within and outside of these worlds." For teachers, professional self-image is also usually balanced with a variety of roles they feel that they have to play (Volkman and Anderson, 1998). This includes all the functional roles a teacher uses while performing his or her duties, what they feel and believe about teaching and being a teacher, and how these are shaped by the teacher's evolving philosophy of teaching (Walkington, 2005). For the purposes of this chapter, teacher role identity indicates the configuration of interpretations that language teachers attach to themselves, as related to the different roles they enact and the different professional activities that they participate in as well as how others see these roles and activities. Some examples of the common roles that have been suggested anecdotally for ESL teacher, but not identified through any research, include teacher as entertainer, cross-cultural expert, oral interviewer, language expert, language model, disciplinarian, counselor, curriculum planner, curriculum evaluator, storyteller, team builder, materials developer, friend, surrogate parent, interaction manager, needs assessor, and joke teller, to name but a few. Much of the recent literature related to teacher professional identity has tended to focus exclusively on novice teachers, both native English-speaking and nonnative English-speaking teachers, but the professional role identities of experienced native English-speaking ESL teachers have not yet received the same attention. However, understanding teacher professional role identity is an important aspect of supporting experienced language teachers as they engage in professional development because these role identities are central to the beliefs, assumptions, values, and practices that guide teacher actions both inside and outside the classroom. This chapter explores the three experienced ESL teachers' roles as revealed after scanning the group discussions and journal writing. A total of 16 main role identities were identified and divided into three major role identity clusters of teacher as manager, teacher as professional, and teacher as "acculturator," the latter of which may be somewhat unique to ESL teachers.

## Teacher roles

Sixteen main professional role identities emerged from the group discussions and these were further placed into three main clusters:

*Teacher as Professional.* In addition, Teacher as Manager was further divided into seven subidentities, teacher as "acculturator" further divided into three subidentities, and Teacher as Professional further divided into three subidentities. The frequency count of the occurrences of each role is also included beside each descriptor. Of course, some of these role identities may overlap and could conceivably be applied in a different cluster; they were placed in a specific cluster because the data suggested that they are the closest representations of these role identities.

## Reflective questions

- Examine the taxonomy above and see what roles you relate to in your current teaching context.
- What is your understanding of the three main clusters?
- What is your understanding of each role?
- Are you surprised by any definitions of any of the roles you see?
- How would you define each role?
- Which cluster would you identify with most and which would you identify with least?
- Which cluster is most surprising for you?
- Which role is most surprising for you?
- Which role is missing for you?

*Table 6.1*  Taxonomy of experienced ESL teacher role identity

| Category | Definition |
| --- | --- |
| Teacher as Manager<br>• *Vendor (12)*<br>• *Entertainer(9)*<br>• *Communication controller (6)*<br>• *Juggler (5)*<br>• *Motivator (4)*<br>• *Presenter (3)*<br>• *Arbitrator(3)* | Attempt to control everything that happens in classroom<br>• A seller of "learning" of English; "selling" a particular teaching method.<br>• Tells jokes and stories to class<br>• Attempt to control classroom communication and classroom interaction dynamics (turn taking etc.)<br>• Multitasker in the classroom<br>• Motivate students to learn; keep students on task<br>• Delivers information<br>• Offers feedback (positive and negative) in classroom |
| Teacher as "acculturator"<br>• *"Socializer"(9)*<br>• *Social Worker (8)*<br>• *Careprovider (4)* | Helps students get accustomed to life outside class<br>• "Socializes" with students; attends functions outside class with students.<br>• Offers advice and support to students on matters related to living in another country/culture<br>• Plays careprovider role for students |
| Teacher as professional<br>• *Collaborator (14)*<br>• *Learner (4)*<br>• *Knowledgeable (3)* | Teachers dedicated to their work; take it seriously<br>• Works and shares with other teachers<br>• Continuously seeks knowledge about teaching and self as teacher<br>• Knowledgeable about teaching and subject matter |

- Can you add more clusters and roles that you consider appropriate for your context?
- Do you think ESL teachers have different roles than teachers of other subjects?

## Teacher as manager

Teacher as manager which had seven subidentities was identified as a role where the teacher is the person attempting to manage what happens within the classroom. Among the more frequently mentioned subidentities within the teacher as manager cluster were teacher as vendor, teacher as entertainer, teacher as communication controller, teacher as juggler, teacher as motivator, teacher as presenter, and teacher as arbitrator.

### Vendor

Teacher as vendor (12 occurrences) is a role used to indicate when a teacher is a seller of the institution, and also to "sell" a particular teaching method. Teacher as vendor as a teacher role for selling the institution

came up in early group discussions that centered on ESL student retention within their institution, and as one teacher noted, "yes, we have
big issues related to student retention here and we basically have to keep
the customers happy." The discussion then centered on the "business of
language education" and the same teacher noted with some discomfort:
"So it comes back to what we really sell, which is often a piece of paper."
Then T2 noted that that even if the customer is not always right, schools
must be aware of the customers, or the students, because their money
affects and attendance affects the whole school: "if administration sees
the numbers and the dollars and that becomes more important than the
learning, not to say that happens with us because I don't think it does. But
you have to be constantly aware of it because it is easy to go that way."

Vendor was also used related to their teaching methods as one teacher
talked about how she had to convince some of her students that a particular approach to writing (the process approach) was "good for them";
to which another teacher responded: "It's like I'm selling you process
writing...buy into it." T2 said that she has now realized that the conflict
of the perception of having to keep the students happy and teaching
them what they need is the real problem for teachers; she said:

> I think there is a big conflict between keeping people happy and
> helping them to learn what they need. It is about balancing that out,
> "what I want you to learn or what I think you need to learn or that
> you expressed a need to learn but now I'm teaching it to you and
> you're not taking it in, you don't seem to want to learn that." That
> conflict. We constantly have that where the needs are supposed to be
> this and they may have even asked for it but when we're actually in
> the delivery of it, they don't want it.

### Entertainer

The role of teacher as entertainer (nine occurrences) suggests a role of
teacher as a performer and/or entertainer. For example, in one group
meeting they all noted that they fear their students will feel the classes
are boring and as one teacher mentioned: "I do find that in ESL that the
expectation for things to be a little bit lively and interesting at certain
points in time comes up quite frequently. The students' expectations
are that they want to have interesting activities and energetic and interesting teachers." To which another teacher replied: "Yeah the biggest
insult you can get would be 'That was so boring.'" The ensuing discussion of this identity role revealed that the teachers suggested they were

constantly keeping in check two different role identity aspects to the job: "entertainment versus learning;" as one teacher noted: "I'm concerned with this balance and do we have to make them happy all the time? Do they always have to be enjoying themselves?"

### Communication controller

The role of teacher as communication controller (six occurrences) was where the teachers saw their role as that of attempting to control classroom communication and classroom interaction dynamics such as in the use of turn taking and pair and group work. As T2 said, "one of the biggest tasks we have as ESL teachers is to get the students talking to each other or generally interacting with each other." T1 also noted that this was her role and especially when trying to establish the sense of turn taking. She said: "I try to establish the idea of turns in speaking classes because some of my students may not be used to taking turns." The group then noted that not all cultures have the same speaking rules when it comes to turn taking.

### Juggler

The role of teacher as juggler (five occurrences) was where the teachers noted all the different tasks they much manage in one day or even one week; as T3 noted: "We are multi-taskers all the time in the classroom." This was a role that was not recognized by the administration who saw then as "just ESL teachers" (T2). As noted in the group discussions this multitasking extended beyond the classroom and this role too was not recognized by their administration. As T3 noted, "not only do I teach them all day, but many times I bring them to the Mall to help them shop while I shop at the same time but there are only so many hours in the day."

### Motivator

Teacher as motivator (four occurrences) was where the teachers attempted to motivate their students to learn in general and when in class, it was specifically a role they suggested where they attempted to keep their students on task. They suggested that this role was a constant and they were used to it. For example, T2 related how she always feels frustrated when some students come to class late or just do not bother to try when they do come to class. T2 said: "they're coming late and they're falling asleep all day ... They want constant stimulation." T2 also said that she tries to motivate her students even when they are taking tests by telling them that her tests only check one aspect of English, and therefore does not reflect the students' complete improvement in English; as she remarked:

> I say, "I know that you're learning English. When I give you a test I'm checking one very particular aspect of that and if you don't do well it doesn't mean that you haven't improved your English. Your English could be improving just fine, beyond my test."

### Presenter

Teacher as presenter (three occurrences) is a role where the teacher delivers information to their students and can be direct presentation or indirect presentation. For direct presentation this role can be in the form of the teacher presenting specific information about language such as grammar rules, writing conventions or other such language details. This role also included assigning different tasks to their students that enable them to learn about language from that task. Regarding indirect presentation T1 remarked that she explains to her students why they are assigned certain tasks so that they understand why they might be difficult and how it is good for language learning:

> More now than in the past, I articulate to my students "This is the reason why we're doing this." Then they seem to take it more if something is really long or it seems really difficult or the topic is not to their liking, at least they know why. I try to tell them why it's going to be good for language learning.

### Arbitrator

Teacher as arbitrator (three occurrences) is where the teachers offer feedback to their students and this feedback can be positive or negative. For example, T2 says she sometimes gives the whole class negative feedback if she thinks they are not trying she continues: "I tell them 'I'm just disappointed in you guys. I expected more of you." But actually I was very strict with them this week because I came down on them and I said, "This is what we're going to be doing for the rest of the term, like or not." In fact, T2 said that she cannot be nice and friendly with her students when they are not doing their job: "So, not coming, not doing their homework. At some point, well that's the end of it. I can't be friendly and nice, and supportive when you're throwing it off for everybody off, that's how I see it."

## Reflective questions

• How would you rank the above roles in terms of importance for you and your context?
• What does "teacher as manager" mean to you?
• What does "teacher as vendor" mean to you?
• Is one of your roles "selling" your institution to those that speak a language other than English?
• If yes, how do you "sell" it?
• Do you feel that you have to "keep the customers happy"? Why or why not?
• How do you keep students "happy" while at the same time providing them with opportunities to learn?
• Do you have to "sell" particular teaching methods or activities to your students?
• What does "teacher as entertainer" mean to you?
• Do you consider yourself an "entertainer" while teaching?
• What does "teacher as juggler" mean to you?
• If you are a "juggler," how do you multitask?
• What does "teacher as motivator" mean to you?
• What does "teacher as presenter" mean to you?
• What does "teacher as arbitrator" mean to you?
• How do you arbitrate when you teach?

### Teacher as "acculturator"

Teacher as "acculturator," a term coined for this study, is used to identify a role where the teacher is seen as one who engages in activities outside the classroom and that help students become accustomed to the local culture. The most frequently occurring subidentities in this cluster were of teacher as "*socializer*" and teacher as *social worker*.

### *Socializer*

Teacher as "socializer" (nine occurrences) indicates where the teacher gets involved with extra activities with students and thus is a "socializer" with students outside of class. For example, in one meeting two of the teachers were discussing the "responsibility" of the teacher to take students out for activities outside the school and the impact this has; as one teacher noted: "I think for the most part, teachers like to be with students. That's what they do. They enjoy being with them." In a later group meeting another teacher noted that they do this voluntary as she said: "The administration almost doesn't even have to make it a structure because teachers love their students, so we do these things. "

*Social worker*

Teacher as social worker (eight occurrences) suggests a role where the teacher offers advice to students just like that of a social worker. One teacher, for example, noted that teaching ESL is similar as "being in a helping profession where you are constantly helping people. I can say, for sure, last year I had at least 5 people crying in my office for various different reasons and not because of me or anything I did." The other teachers had similar experiences about spending time with students outside of class listening to their problems; as another teacher noted: "I would be the first one, to sit down and let the students talk and cry because I am implicitly a helper, that's just who I am and I just have to fix it [whatever problem the students have], because I know that get my energy from people."

### Reflective questions

- How would you rank the above roles in terms of importance for you and your context?
- What does teacher as "acculturator" mean to you?
- Do you think the term "acculturator" is unique to those who teach English to speakers of other languages? Why or why not?
- Do you think ESL teachers must go beyond the classroom to help their students?
- What does "teacher as socializer" mean to you?
- Do you socialize with your students? If yes, how? If not, why not?
- What does "teacher as social worker" mean to you?
- Do you think ESL teachers are social workers? If yes, how? If not, why not?

### Teacher as professional

Teacher as professional role was identified where the teacher is seen as one who is dedicated to her work, and takes it very seriously. The most frequently occurring subidentities in this cluster were teacher as *collaborator*, and teacher as *learner*.

*Collaborator*

Teacher as collaborator (14 occurrences), the most frequent role that emerged in all the group meetings, is where a teacher collaborates and shares with other teachers and gives advice to other ESL teachers. For example, one teacher talked about working with an ESL teacher in the same institution (but outside this teacher group) about her struggles teaching the same level class and she realized that as a result of her discussions she saw her colleague "in a whole new role" as her colleague, "clicked into almost a mentor mode because she had taught speaking so much more than I have recently and then she came up with these [teaching] ideas." This reflection made her realize the value of colleagues collaborating; she continued: "It just started to hit me that as we were taking that we could do more together than this; that's what you need between colleagues to get this kind of thing going." Another teacher in the group also noted the value of collaborating with colleagues when she wanted to share her findings of a survey she performed with her students regarding her teaching; she continued: "I'm meeting with other teachers and we're talking about our teaching. We're trying to become better teachers. I like to share what I learn with them."

*Learner*

Teacher as learner (four occurrences) was identified for a teacher who continually seeks knowledge about teaching and/or themselves as teachers. For example one teacher reflected on her "thirst for gaining knowledge" about teaching and herself and remarked: "I am one of those teachers that will sign up for any workshop or conference and devour the professional magazines that come in to the office. I often chat about my classes and teaching and share ideas with my colleagues of choice for that kind of thing. Simply, I enjoy it."

## Reflective questions

- How would you rank the above roles in terms of importance for you and your context?
- What does "teacher as professional" mean to you?
- Are all ESL teachers considered "professional"?
- What does "teacher as collaborator" mean to you?
- Do you collaborate with your colleagues and institution? If yes, how? If not, why not?
- What does "teacher as learner" mean to you?
- Are you still a learner even though you are an experienced teacher? If yes, how do you "learn"?
- Do you think all experienced ESL teachers are still learning?
- What does "teacher as knowledgeable" mean to you?
- Do you think "teacher as knowledgeable" is in conflict with "teacher as learner"?

## Readymade or imposed teacher roles?

Some roles are taken on and some roles are given to us by others. So a central question related to role identity that is pertinent to the above taxonomy outlined in Table 6.1 is whether these roles have been predetermined (given by others) or individually constructed (taken on either consciously or subconsciously) by the teachers. In other words, do they just fit into these roles by following preexisting patterns, or have these roles developed over time through their interactions with other teachers? The difference between these two positions (imposed roles as opposed to roles taken on by teachers) is really one of what can be perceived as being *readymade* roles versus *individually created* roles that have been negotiated over time. No doubt some roles also fall in between so we really talk about a continuum of readymade roles at one end and individually created roles on the other end. Examples of readymade identity roles that emerged from the group discussions would include teacher as *vendor*, *entertainer*, and *care provider*. It is clear that none of the three teachers were comfortable with their role as teacher as vendor when it came to their role in student retention and as a result of their reflection on the findings outlined in this paper realized that this was an institutionally created readymade role rather than an individually created or negotiated identity role. The issue of student retention discussed earlier was an uneasy one for these three experienced ESL teachers because all were well aware of the tension between the need for quality ESL education to make sure their students survive and excel not only in other courses within their institution but also in the wider community, and the institution's need to move the international students into other programs in the institution. One administrator explained the function and role of the ESL Department in the institution as follows: "The function of the ESL team/ department is primarily to make sure that we offer a strong English for Academic Purposes program, so that as many as possible of our international ESL students continue at the college in regular diploma/graduate certificate/applied degree programs." However, as stated earlier they also feel a certain amount of pressure to balance this issue of retention and education; as one teacher again noted: "I feel that that pressure is there. I mean we work in a very good place in terms of, you know trying to balance out an education and learning, learning is important. But it starts to trigger that sense of we've got to keep the customers happy. We've got to keep them paying their money and that kind of thing."

Also, all three teachers seemed to be uncomfortable with teacher as entertainer role and described this with equal emotionally laden terms as that of teacher as vendor. They definitely do not embrace these roles and they seem thrust upon them possibly by the administration (vendor for student retention), and their students (vendor as seller of learning and entertainer). However in postreflection interviews directly related to the entertainer role identity, one teacher noted that the role of entertainer can be combined with teacher as motivator because "in the final analysis this is why teachers feel they must entertain: in order to motivate their students to learn more." It is possible too that teacher as care provider further explained by the teachers as linked to gender in terms of taking on a caring role for their students could also be thrust upon them by their students. Indeed the terms mother or motherly were used by all three in the discourse of the meetings and linked to a mother's role such as getting their "children" (i.e. students) to do their homework, and enforcing other such motherly roles to get young "children" to accomplish various learning tasks.

It is quite possible too that the role identity cluster teacher as "acculturator" with teacher as "*socializer*," *social worker*, and *motherly* may also be considered a readymade identity role as the teachers did not actively seek out these roles although they also all agreed that this is part of their job as an ESL teacher. The role identity cluster of teacher as "acculturator" finding supports Duff and Uchida's (1997: 476) findings about language teachers as cultural workers: "Whether they are aware of it or not, language teachers are very much involved in the transmission of culture, and each selection of videos, newspaper clippings, seating plans, activities, and so on has social, cultural, and educational significance." This role identity cluster brings ESL teachers in closer proximity to their students than would probably normally be the case for teachers of other subjects such as math or science. Indeed, as Hawkins and Norton (2009: 32) have also recently noted, "language teachers are often the first contacts that newcomers (immigrants, migrants, and refugees) have in the target language community, and they serve as social mediators and informants in the new environment." As such language teachers continue to "play a key role in the construction of the learners' views of their homes; their understandings of unfamiliar belief systems, values and practices; and their negotiations of new social relationships" (Hawkins and Norton, 2009: 32). Indeed, it is quite possible that this identity cluster finding is what makes TESOL professionals unique as teachers and may not be a similar "benchmark" for teachers of other subjects as is the case for the other two clusters *teacher as manager* and *teacher as professional*, which can be applicable to the teaching of all subject areas.

Teacher as *collaborator, knowledgeable,* and *learner* can be seen as examples of roles that can be considered individually created and negotiated (these can also be structured in a top-down mode by the administration in many institutions) identity roles because all three teachers actively seek out situations in which they can collaborate and situations in which they can further develop themselves as teachers such as joining the teacher development group that this study reports on. Teacher as *communication controller, juggler, motivator, presenter,* and *arbitrator* are also examples of individually created identity roles as each teacher negotiates these roles in their own individual and creative ways. For example, no two teachers in the group will arbitrate in the same way nor will any try to control classroom communication and interaction in the same way nor juggle, engage or motivate their students in the same ways. That said, it is not easy to distinguish about the degree to which identity roles are either predetermined or negotiated through interaction and this is why as, Cohen (2008: 18) has noted, that the notion of role identity offers a useful analytic tool for addressing the complexity of teachers' identity experiences, because it "highlights the tension between received expectations and individual negotiation that is at the heart of teacher identity."

Any discussion of professional role identity must also include the concept of "self" as an essential consideration (Beijard, Meijer, and Verloop, 2004); however, teachers' conceptualizations of their self-image and the various roles they play are usually held at the tacit level of awareness. As such, "reflection" is seen as a key component associated with understanding the concept of "self" because it brings these tacit conceptualizations to level of awareness (Farrell, 2007). As Beijard et al. (2004: 114) point out, for teachers "it is impossible to speak about the 'self' when there is no reflection." Through self-reflection then teachers can relate their experiences to their beliefs, knowledge, and emotions in order to as Beijard et al. (2004: 114) have noted, "to integrate what is socially relevant into their images of themselves as teachers." It is important too for second language teachers to be able to bring these role identities to the level of awareness so that they can as Leung (2009: 53) has recently noted, become "engaged in reflexive examination of their own beliefs and action." However, it is not usually the case that experienced ESL teachers readily consciously reflect on the different role identities they hold, or may have been ascribed, and so the research reported in this paper is one attempt to accommodate these reflections. Consequently, for experienced ESL teachers in mid-career, opportunities must be made for them to become more aware of their role identity and this is best encouraged through reflective practice (see

Farrell, 2007, 2013). Regular discussions in a teacher group, similar to what occurred in this study, seems to be a useful way of releasing teachers from the isolation of their classrooms so that they can consciously explore their identity roles as part of their ongoing professional development. Teachers can articulate these roles through their biographies, stories, and/or diaries and share with other teachers as they begin to construct and reconstruct their teaching worlds.

## Reflective questions

- Why is the concept of "self" important to consider when reflecting on a teacher's role?
- Why do you think teachers do not generally consciously reflect on the roles they are given or the roles they take on?
- How does reflecting on a teacher's role reveal the complexity of a language teacher's work?
- How do the various roles outlined in this chapter indicate the complexity of language teaching?
- Do you reflect on your various roles as a teacher?
- If yes, what are these roles and if no, why not?
- Which of these roles did you choose?
- Which of these roles were you "given" by the institution and/or your colleagues?
- Do you think your school/institution imposes any roles on you as a teacher?
- If you have roles imposed on you by the institution, which of them do you think are not in your interests?
- Why do you think the role "teacher as acculturator" bring ESL teachers in closer proximity to their students than would normally be the case for teachers of other subjects?

## Teachers' reflections on roles

After the period of reflection I asked all three teachers to suggest roles or metaphors for their understanding of teaching and learning now that they had finished reflecting on their practice after a period of two years. T2 now suggested that "an ESL teacher is like the machine in a batting cage". She continued:

> The teacher continuously (and in controlled fashion of course!) lobs language information and opportunities to use language at the

students, who then decide how much they will put into taking a swing at improving their ability.

Her metaphor for her students was a "little child." T2 continued:

> An ESL student is like a little child who isn't completely sure he or she wants to be fed. Imagine the parent holding the spoon of food, trying to coax the child into opening his mouth and eating. The child likes the idea of food/learning a language, but may need convincing that many different ways of learning can all be good, not just the favorite one.

I then asked her about a metaphor she would use for her classroom and she said:

> An ESL classroom can be like a beehive. It's a busy place where the students and teacher alike are working for the same reason. It takes work on the part of all the members to build relationships and achieve a common goal. When students head out of the class, they collect knowledge and experiences that they can bring back to the hive to enrich the environment.

I then asked her what metaphor she would use for learning English and she said that learning English as a second language "is like wandering through a city like Venice." She continued:

> You start off thinking that you know where you want to go, but there is never a direct route, an every time you turn a corner/learn something new, you find something new and interesting and end up learning more than you had originally planned.

T1 said that an ESL teacher is like a "gardener." An ESL student is like a "plant/flower/ and also the gardener too." She said an ESL classroom is like a "garden." T1 also noted that learning a second language is like "gardening" and entails a whole variety of preconditions to come together. She continued: "It is a combination of science and art. Some things we can control and manage and others we can't. Then you just have to let it happen, if it wants to."

## Reflective questions

- What is your understanding of teacher like "the machine in a batting cage"?

- What is your understanding of student as a "little child"?
- What is your understanding of classroom "like a beehive"?
- What is your understanding of learning English as a second language "like wandering through a city like Venice"?
- What is your understanding of T1's metaphor of teacher as gardener, students like plants and classroom as a garden?

By reflecting on their roles and metaphors, teachers are able to discover what positive and negative influences they may have on the classroom and the students, or as one of the teachers noticed: "I get to the point where you actually do see the gloss over their eyes" and how they can improve as language teachers and human beings: "learning to teach over my career has been a very, very, very huge learning curve." Secondly, the implications of metaphors like these also allow teachers to understand how they might be seen through the eyes of a student. Taking a step back and looking through the eyes of another person is an excellent way to self-reflect and try and see oneself from a different perspective (e.g. as T2 noticed when using metaphors that she may not always do herself what she asks her students to do: "I'm not practicing what I preach"). These expressions can also indicate how much of an influence an individual's personality (see also Chapter 5 on teacher beliefs on the role of personality on classroom decision making) has on what they do and in what manner they do things. For example, a teacher might be able to look at the metaphors generated from their discussions about teaching and see whether or not the way they behave in the classroom matches their "real-life" personality. It may be common for a teacher, or anyone taking part in the language learning process, to adapt and alter their personality to fit the style and needs of a class or student. Though this may be useful at times, many teachers (and students) want to "be themselves" and want their teaching to reflect their personalities. When there is a gap between who they are in and out of the classroom, often at this point teaching becomes tiresome because the teacher is not only working, but also being a different person. By looking at these expressions and metaphors, potentially a teacher can reflect on their "classroom personality(s)" and see whether or not it matches their "real-life" personality.

### Reflective questions

- Metaphors can used to reveal a teacher's set of beliefs. How can they reveal these beliefs?

- Metaphors are also an important part of teachers' personal practical knowledge that shapes their understanding of their role as teachers. Why do you think this is the case?
- Finish this statement: "An English language teacher is _____."
- Finish this statement: "A language student is _____."
- Finish these statements:
  - "A good second language teacher is _____."
  - "A good second language student is _____."
- Has your use of metaphors changed over time since you became a language teacher?
  - If yes, what differences have you noticed?
  - What experiences have led to the change you noticed?
  - If no changes have occurred in your metaphor usage, what experiences have resulted in this confirmation of your original metaphor usage?
- Do you think male teachers will use different metaphors for teaching and learning than female teachers?
- Would you use similar or different metaphors than the teachers in this study, who were all females, used?
- What were the most "unusual" metaphors the teachers in this study used in your opinion and why?
- Some scholars say that the real test of the teachers' metaphor usage is not whether they are "right or wrong" according to an outsider's perceptions, but the extent to which they are useful for the teacher. Do you think there are some "right" and "wrong" metaphors that the teachers in this study used? Explain your answer.

Metaphors define values by the tone and directness of a comment made by a teacher or student. A teacher who would implicitly mention metaphors valuing the importance of the teacher as a nurturer would value the notion that students constantly need help and the role of a teacher includes this. A teacher who often uses metaphors of power to describe themselves places value on strictness and classroom management. Lastly, metaphors also define classroom interaction and knowledge, as seen through the various examples portraying the teacher as a conduit of knowledge, a gatekeeper to knowledge, and a repeater of knowledge. By analyzing teachers' metaphors, one can shine a light on their belief and value of the teacher being the one in control of the class and directing their knowledge into the minds of their students.

## Conclusion

Burns and Richards (2009: 5) have suggested that role identity "reflects how individuals see themselves and how they enact their *roles* [emphasis added] within different settings." Role identities, according to Cohen (2008: 832), are "powerful organizing structures because people get recognition, positive reinforcement from others, and other rewards when they accomplish roles successfully." When language teachers consciously reflect on the various roles (in terms of metaphors) they take on or are given to them by their institutions, colleagues or others they can start the process of trying to figure out who they are and who they want to become as they continue their careers as reflective practitioners. This chapter also suggested that reflecting on metaphor usage can reveal a teacher's teaching philosophy and belief system and when then teachers can decide if these metaphors still hold true for their present context and conditions of teaching. They can be challenged as to their current relevance and then they can begin to develop alternative and more appropriate metaphors that best represent their practice if they so desire. This is important because when challenged, the teacher makes the decision rather than following previously held beliefs that have been entrenched over time.

# 7
# Reflection on Critical Incidents

## Introduction

After many years of teaching, some ESL teachers can feel a sense of isolation because they are but one person in a room with 20 or more students and as such many have a difficult time reflecting on their practice. However, the use of narratives for self-reflection offers these teachers "a safe and nonjudgmental support system for sharing the emotional stresses and isolating experiences of the classroom" (Jalongo and Isenberg, 1995: 162). McCabe (2002) suggests that stories can set off a dialogue about teaching that can offer strategies for dealing with problems many teachers may face as well as the successes they manage. Teachers can reflect on their practice by articulating their stories to themselves or others because these stories reveal the "knowledge, ideas, perspectives, understandings, and experiences that guide their work" (Johnson and Golombek, 2002: 7). By telling their stories, teachers can make better sense of seemingly random experiences because they hold the inside knowledge, especially personal intuitive knowledge, expertise, and experience that is based on their accumulated years as language educators teaching in schools and classrooms. These self-reflective stories can provide a rich source of teacher-generated information that allows them to reflect on how they got where they are today, how they conduct practice, the thinking and problem-solving they employ during their practice, and their underlying assumptions, values and beliefs that have ruled their past and current practices. That said, Bell (2002) has suggested that narrative reflection goes beyond language teachers just simply telling stories about general happenings within their teaching world without much of a focus; in other words it is not just sitting around the camp fire telling stories for fun. For narrative reflection to be really beneficial to teachers, it should also feature recounts of specific classroom events and experiences such as incidents that teachers deem critical for their professional development. Thus, narrative inquiry as it is outlined in this chapter is grounded in John Dewey's (1933) notion of reflecting on teachers' specific (rather than general) experiences, because we must remember that a teacher's life is itself a narrative of the composite of these critical incidents and experiences. This chapter explores the sources of three experienced ESL teachers' critical incidents as revealed after scanning the group discussions and journal writing that were held over the two-year period. I also adapted McCabe's (2002) framework for analyzing the narratives that the critical incidents emerged from as follows:

• *Orientation*: This part answers the following questions: Who? When? What? Where?
• *Complication*: Outlines what happened and the problem that occurred along with any turning point in the story.
• *Evaluation:* This part answers the question: So what? What this means for the participants in the story.
• *Result*: This part outlines and explains the resolution to the problem/ crisis.

## Critical incident I: *negative feedback*

The following teacher narrative, as told (in the teacher's own words) by one of teachers from the teacher reflection group, outlines the details of a critical incident that can be identified as "negative feedback" (Farrell, 2007). Specifically, the case study details her concerns of the "negative feedback" she reported to have received from one of her students after one of her classes. The information about the critical incident comes from a combination of teacher journal entries the teacher wrote and what she reported about the incident to the other teachers in the teacher reflection group during group meetings. The narrative is presented in the teacher's own words so as to provide as much reality as possible.

### Orientation

I was teaching a course entitled *Socio-cultural Influences on Teaching English as a Second Language*. It was in the autumn term; 3 hours per week; most were university graduates who wanted to become ESL/EFL teachers. I decided to give the students a survey about the class. The survey is called the Key Performance Indicators (KPI) and it is done across the province by all colleges. It is the primary source of information about the course and we are held accountable for the responses. For example, in previous years, there was a very low part of our KPIs related to college facilities and we, as a department, had to hold a focus group discussion with our students to better understand their responses. We discussed it with our program advisory committee, and the program chair had to come up with strategies for improvement. It asks students to comment on a very wide range of things from the actual learning experience and program quality to college resources, facilities, technology, cafeteria/bookstore, skills for future career, right down to teacher punctuality. They complete it at the end of the program. Not all courses in a program have to do it every term and not all programs necessarily do one every year. Because it is so extensive, they take a cross section of programs in the college. It is the type where a statement is given and the students can mark their answer on a continuum: Agree strongly, agree, neither agree nor disagree, disagree, disagree strongly. When we did our official surveys they give you the bar graph or the percentages showing, you know disagreed, neutral, and then agree. Seven percent were always that disagree, which indicates out of a class, 19 students or whatever, that one person hated everything in my class.

## Complication

The student in this incident was one who had repeatedly, from the very first class, demonstrated a contemptuous boredom with the program as a whole. He had indicated this in a number of ways to all his teachers. In person, he was tactfully polite, but in his written assignments, he would express his truer feelings. He always seemed to resist or think he was above what we were teaching in the program. We suspected that his fiancée, who was also in the program, had dragged him there so that they could travel overseas together. He had just completed university and seemed to think he was above a college program; although, this is now my own perception, as I seek to understand why someone would stay in a program that he clearly didn't like. Because the negative feedback came from this student, I could have dismissed it more easily ... it was predictable; of course he didn't like anything. It was really not a surprise. And yet, I still felt the sting of the negative result and comments and had to reflect upon why.

## Evaluation

I was very disturbed by unsolicited comments from this student at the end of December. Even after all our talk about feedback from students and our ability to take feedback and make changes, and not taking it personally, I was amazed by my hugely, negative, emotional response. Just when you think you're above the fray, some negative feedback hits you between the eyes. After doing some thinking on the experience, I have come to realize that it wasn't the comment itself that disturbed me (basically because I knew it was not valid), but the fact that this student felt he had a right to criticize the course content (and indirectly me) despite the fact that he had not attended a significant portion of the course and actually failed the final exam. The fact is that I felt vulnerable. I think I was worried that someone (other teachers? not sure) was going to listen to this guy and that judgments would be made about this course and about me.

### Result

I'm totally over that now. In fact, I think I am probably a more severe critic of myself than anyone else could be. I wasn't concerned by the positives or the negatives or the neutrals. I mean, I looked at them and it was interesting and there were not really surprising things but I knew that was him and it was like, oh well.

Critical incidents can be classified as being positive or negative events and may be identified by reflecting on a "teaching high" or a "teaching low" (Thiel, 1999). A teaching high in a language class could be a sudden change in the lesson plan teachers makes during class because of their perceptions of the current events. They, then, decide to alter the events and this change, in turn, has some positive overall effect on the lesson such as more student response. A teaching low could be a specific classroom incident that is immediately problematic or puzzling for the teacher, such as one student suddenly crying during class for no apparent reason. The incident reported on here could be classified as a teaching "low" for the teacher because the negative comments provided by the student went beyond what the teacher was expecting. As such the self-reflective narrative (in the form of a critical incident) outlined demonstrates how real practices (also note the use of the teacher's own words throughout) can conflict with expectations and outcomes. However, as McCabe (2002: 83) recommends, when we begin to analyze such critical incidents in which outcomes conflict with our expectations, "we can come to a greater understanding of the expectations themselves—what our beliefs, philosophies, understandings, conceptions (of the classroom, of the language, of the students, of ourselves) actually are." Indeed, by vividly recalling and describing such critical incidents, teachers can begin to explore all kinds of assumptions that underlie their practice. This was the situation for the teacher reflecting on the critical incident I. By reflecting and analyzing the critical incident outlined above, the teacher gained a greater awareness of herself as a teacher and her practices, which is one of the main goals of reflective practice. She also became more empowered as a result of telling her story and then reflecting on it; as she commented after reading her own story: "So I feel empowered by our PD (professional development)."

## Reflective questions

- Comment on each phase of this particular incident before moving onto the following phase.
- Describe a recent "teaching high" you experienced.
- Describe a recent "teaching low" you experienced.
- In the "evaluation" section why do you think the teacher was "amazed by my hugely, negative, emotional response" to the student?
- Do you think that students have the right to criticize the course content?
- In the 'results' section the teacher says that she is "a more severe critic" of herself than anyone else could be. Do you think teachers are generally hard on themselves than others would be?
- Do you tend to a sever critic of yourself as a teacher?
- How long would it take for you to "get over" this incident?
- McCabe (2002: 89) suggests that analysis of critical incidents can "lead to further exploration of different aspects of teaching through action research." Use the above incident as a possible starting point for an action research project of your own on how you giving feedback in your classes.

## Critical incident II: *evaluation and feedback*

The second incident, related to the first one above, reports on a teacher narrative as told by another of teachers from the teacher reflection group. Again, the information about the critical incident comes from a combination of a journal entry she made and what she said about the incident in a group meeting. Specifically, the incident details her concerns of the "Evaluation and Feedback" she reported when she was teaching a TESL course. The narrative is presented in the teacher's own words and used McCabe's (2002) framework to outline and analyze the incident.

### Orientation

In my teaching English as a second language (TESL) class, one of the assessed tasks is called "peer teaching." The pre-service teachers present their lesson plan (another assessed task) to the class and teaches one or two of the activities or techniques in "teacher-mode" with us role playing being ESL learners, according to the class profile they have indicated on their lesson plan. Having done this in my TESL classes numerous times, I feel there is a certain value in sharing the lesson plans they have made while they are trying out their teaching skills. I have an evaluation scheme that assesses the following: use of language, classroom management, knowledge of technique, visual aid, organization, and presentation skills. The students know from the second day of classes that this is coming at the end of the term, I model the task for them and I give them their lesson plan feedback back before they peer teach. I do everything possible to prepare them and make them comfortable but it still can be slightly stressful for them. To be expected I guess.

## Complication

Now to the problem: evaluation and giving feedback. I have, in the past, had to give people feedback about their lessons that they are not happy with, in other words, criticism. Trust me, I do this in the kindest softest way I can. This week a particular pre-service teacher was not very successful in his peer teaching. This student has been "a question mark" since the beginning of the term. He is intelligent and expresses himself well on paper and understands the theoretical concepts. His written work has been excellent. He is just not a clear communicator in front of the class. I should also mention his overall score was not too bad. I felt I was perhaps overly generous in some areas. I had to give him this critical feedback along with some positive feedback. That was fine for me but he was upset by it. I also had to give him a numerical grade using my scoring key. In the end I realize this is his issue and that he needs to behave in a more professional manner. I was not that hard on him.

## Evaluation

I now have a number of questions on this issue:

- Should I give the feedback in a different way? How can I improve in how I do it?
- Some people accept and enjoy receiving my feedback and see the purpose of why I am doing this while others take it too personally or see it as a personal attack (which it is not)?
- How do I deal with the opposing goals of supportive feedback and evaluation for grades? Should I stop evaluating the peer teaching and just use it as an opportunity for feedback?

- How can I ensure that all my pre-service teachers see that I am trying to help them not hinder them?
- How do I react when I am criticized?
- Am I so understanding of criticism?
- Why is it when giving ESL presentation feedback I do not have as much difficulty?
- How is it different, for example, after a speaking presentation?
- If a person is not good in front of the class and may not be successful in the ESL teaching classroom because of it, isn't it partially my responsibility to guide them into reflection and improving and perhaps I just do not like have this responsibility?

When an ESL student takes my feedback overly personally, I do not worry about it too much. I feel that someone who is about to become a teacher needs to know when they are getting constructive criticism and how not to take it too personally. As a teacher I get criticized regularly from a variety of sources.

### Result

I always start my feedback sessions, and I did with him, the "problem" teacher as well, something like "How do you think it went?" Or "How did you feel?" And then he said, he didn't really respond very much to that. I remember that he didn't say anything. And then I kind of probed further and asked him "Were you a bit nervous?" And then he said, "No. Well, maybe a little." He's one of these people, very hard to communicate with. He's never been a teacher. So there were issues with his lesson plan prior to going into this so I think he was already hyped up. And he's been following me around like a little lost puppy all term. "Okay, this is what I'm going to do with my lesson plan." And I'm like, whatever you want to do. It's your lesson plan. I'm trying not to do it for them. He'd say, "What if I do this? What if I do that?" I would say, I don't know. I'll have to see, you know when the lesson plan is handed in I'll see how it all hangs together and see if it works, so highly needy. I have a scoring key: it's split up into different sections and then it's broken down even further and they get little check marks with it and then the numbers come in, which I hate.

Then I write comments on the side and then for each section they get a grade out of 10 which all adds up in the end. His overall score, I always start with the overall score and say, "Overall, this is what I've given you," so at least they have a sense of where we're heading in. And for the most part, most people get very high marks, I don't expect them to be perfection. I'm thinking half-way through the program do I see someone who is developing at the half-way mark and in some cases he was. He got, you know a few 10 out of 10 in there. But this is where I had the problem with the feedback because I can't tell him directly, you have a speech impediment. This is the problem, partially the problem. And when he's nervous he speeds up and that's where it comes out the most, which is why I asked him if he was nervous. When he's nervous and he starts to speak quickly, he starts to stumble over his words and he mumbles. His pronunciation loses its clarity. He's not enunciating words. I can't identify it exactly. It's not quite disfluency. He's not stuttering or anything like that but it's bordering on it, which is a concern for someone going into the language teaching profession, which I said from day one. When he switched into teacher's mode, he actually slowed down and was quite clear so this helped him somewhat. There were also a number of different issues with the classroom management that, you know came up. But that's where he got quite defensive. I told him, I said, "In an ESL class the students are not going to automatically repair that for you. They are just going to look around and they are going to be confused. They are going to have that piece of paper and they are not going to have a clue what to do. They are not going to say, 'Okay. Well, let's just role play with our cup.' They are not going to do that." So he kept saying "I would have...I had that in my lesson plan...I wrote it down that I would do that but I didn't do that." I said to him that it's not what you would have done but what you did do. I gave him his overall grade: 38 out of 60, yeah, he passes. You need to have an overall grade of 50 in our program to pass. With his other grades, all his written work is excellent.

## Reflective questions

- In the "evaluation" phase above the teacher asks a number of questions before making a short evaluation. Try to answer each of these questions yourself:
  - Should I give the feedback in a different way? How can I improve in how I do it?
  - Some people accept and enjoy receiving my feedback and see the purpose of why I am doing this while others take it too personally or see it as a personal attack (which it is not)?
  - How do I deal with the opposing goals of supportive feedback and evaluation for grades? Should I stop evaluating the peer teaching and just use it as an opportunity for feedback?

- How can I ensure that all my pre-service teachers see that I am trying to help them not hinder them?
- How do I react when I am criticized?
- Am I so understanding of criticism?
- Why is it when giving ESL presentation feedback I do not have as much difficulty?
- How is it different, for example, after a speaking presentation?
- If a person is not good in front of the class and may not be successful in the ESL teaching classroom because of it, isn't it partially my responsibility to guide them into reflection and improving and perhaps I just do not like have this responsibility?

- In the 'results' section the teacher says the student has a speech issue but that she cannot really identify the problem. What is your understanding of this issue?
- The teacher says: "He's not stuttering or anything like that but it's bordering on it, which is a concern for someone going into the language teaching profession." Do you think that language teachers could have a problem teaching if they have some speech problem?
- She then noted that when he switched into teacher's mode "he actually slowed down and was quite clear so this helped him somewhat." What is your understanding of this development?
- What is your understanding of this critical incident?

## Critical incidents: delayed reflection

The two critical incidents reported on in this chapter are what would be considered negative and "teaching lows." So it may be an idea when encouraging teachers to reflect on critical incidents, to have them write two "incidents": one should be a teaching high (because teachers tend to focus only on what goes "wrong" and forget to focus on what goes "well") and the other a teaching low. They should avoid writing explanations and interpretations at this first stage and just include all the details as contained in an *orientation* as outlined in the case study above (e.g. focus only on the *what, where, when, who*). On a separate page, teachers can attempt to explain and interpret the incident. Incidents only really become critical when they are subject to this conscious reflection, and when language teachers formally analyze these critical incidents, they can uncover new understandings of their practice. Thus, when a critical incident occurs, it interrupts (or highlights) the taken for granted ways of thinking about teaching, and, by analyzing such incidents, teachers can examine the values and beliefs that underpin their perceptions about teaching (Farrell, 2007). Richards and Farrell (2005) suggest that teachers may want to consider what happened directly before and after each incident as well as the teacher's reactions at the time of the incident. In this way, they suggest that teachers may be able to unpack their underlying assumptions about teaching and learning English language.

Of course, teachers can also fully adapt McCabe's (2002) framework as outlined in this chapter as a means of analyzing their incidents: orientation, complication, evaluation, result. In order to follow this framework, teachers should be fully aware of the importance of each stage of the framework and not to try to skip any stage. Regardless of the exact method of organizing critical incidents, Thiel (1999) suggests that the reporting of critical incidents (written or spoken) should have at the very least the following four steps:

- Self-observation—identify significant events that occur in the classroom.
- Detailed written description of what happened—the incident itself, what led up to it and what followed.
- Self-awareness—analyze why the incident happened.
- Self-evaluation—consider how the incident led to a change in understanding of teaching.

In order to get the most out of this reflective process, teachers should team up with another teacher, sometimes called a critical friend. A critical friendship is where a trusted colleague gives advice to a teacher as a friend rather than a consultant in order to develop the reflective abilities of the teacher who is conducting his or her own reflections. They can exchange the first page details of the incidents with each other and then suggest interpretations for the incidents. The critical friend's interpretations can later be compared with the interpretations already constructed by the teacher who experienced the incident and any new meaning to the original incident can be added. Reflecting on critical incidents in this manner with a critical friend (or with a group of teachers) can be a good example of the old adage of "two heads are better than one."

## Reflective questions

- Write a narrative of two "incidents" that you consider critical from their practice. One should be a teaching high (because teachers tend to focus only on what goes "wrong" and forget to focus on what goes "well") and the other a teaching low. Avoid writing explanations and interpretations at this first stage and just include all the details as contained in an *orientation* as outlined in the above (e.g. focus only on the *what, where, when, who*) above.

- On a separate page, attempt to explain and interpret the incident. You may want to consider what happened directly before and after each incident as well as the teacher's reactions at the time of the incident.
- Now try to use McCabe's (2002) framework as outlined in this chapter as a means of analyzing their incidents: orientation, complication, evaluation, result.
- Compare this framework with what you did in the first two steps and decide which was best for you.

## Conclusion

This chapter has suggested that language teachers can choose from various different means of "imposing order" (Johnson and Golombek, 2002: 4) on their seemingly disparate practices such as analyzing critical incidents that occur in their practice. In addition, the incidents outline how teacher-generated critical incidents can offer a rich source of information about how experienced ESL teachers actually conduct their practices: the thinking and problem-solving they employ, and their underlying assumptions, values, and beliefs. By detailing, analyzing and interpreting important critical incidents, ESL teachers are provided with further opportunities to reflect on and consolidate their philosophical and theoretical understanding of their practices and if they desire, can even lead to further and more detailed exploration of different aspects of teaching through detailed action research projects.

# 8
# Resisting Plateauing through Teacher Reflection Groups

## Introduction

As mentioned previously teachers, as well as those in most professions, go through different career cycles throughout their careers. There is probably no one route within these cycles that all teachers take as they traverse their teaching careers and especially with TESOL, where there is so much variance in settings and contexts where programs are delivered (e.g. English as a second language, English as a foreign language, English as an international language, to name but a few). Some teachers may stay at one or more particular stages for different reasons but it is safe to say that some experienced language teachers, especially in mid-career, may encounter a period where they feel they are not "progressing" toward any tangible career goal. In many cases this can be perceived as a fuzzy feeling of sorts, or even depression that teachers may relate to burnout of some sort. While burnout is a real possibility for some teachers, it also may be that these teachers have reached that plateau where they cannot see their future as language teachers and note as one of the teachers in the teacher reflection group reported at the beginning of their period of reflection: "gone a little stale." This teacher continued: "I'd like to have some scheduled, committed time to take stock of how I'm doing in the classroom for both me and my students." All three teachers decided to take action about their own feelings of reaching a place in their professional lives where they needed to take stock (indeed one teacher even used the word "plateauing") and asked this author to act as facilitator for their teacher reflection group as they reflected on their practice.

This chapter outlines how language teachers can consider their professional development through the lens of a teacher reflection group where they gather with a group of colleagues who may have "perceived their career to be at a standstill," and "void of new challenges" (Meister and Ahrens, 2011:773) so that they can learn how to understand, confront, and eventually resist plateauing. Indeed, teachers can join a teacher reflection group even if they are not plateauing so as to be able to interact with colleagues in an informal manner and to support each other and receive support from the group so that they can resist burnout and plateauing before they happen. One way of counteracting teacher plateauing is by first understanding it more and thus being able to recognizing it for what it is. As such, this chapter first discussed the concept of teacher plateauing and then provides a framework for teacher reflection groups so that language teachers can engage in professional development through reflective practice.

## Causes of plateauing

The results of the group discussions (Chapter 3) and their journal writing (Chapter 4) suggest that two of the main factors that contributed to the three teachers reaching a career plateau were a recognition of the "front-loaded" nature of teaching and a resulting lack of career advancement, and teacher longevity, similar findings to what other scholars in general education studies have reported (e.g. Milstein, 1990; Meister and Ahrens, 2011). The three ESL teachers realized that they were teaching in an institution during their mid-career phase with few (if any) chances for promotion. Their lack of promotional opportunities were most likely related to the front-loaded nature of teaching where all three teachers were tenured with no career ladder left for them to climb. T1 attempted to counteract this lack of advancement but did not want to leave the classroom completely. So she attempted to combine her regular teaching with some administrative work by taking on an extra role as ESL course director. She soon discovered, however, that this extra administrative position was actually detrimental to her career and even her health. During the two-year period of this study she realized that she was having great difficulty trying to balance her work and her personal life and so as a result many of the group discussions, she decided to give up this administrative position and said that she felt better as a result.

One of the career frustrations that all three teachers noted was the negative impact of the testing regime that they imposed on the teachers by the administration to ensure the ESL students moved quickly into the main college programs after their English language instruction, and how this adversely affected their morale. As T2 mentioned, "we basically have to keep the customers happy." This issue may be unique to

TESOL professionals working in similar institutions where administrators give conditional acceptance to content courses and if they do not succeed in getting their students to reach levels of English proficiency, may be viewed as unrealistically ineffective as a result. In other words, this puts added pressure on them to achieve something that may be in fact unachievable especially with students who do not try or are just not able to succeed. So administrations need to be more aware of these unique duties and roles ESL teachers play within their institutions.

The administration in an institution thus has an important role to play in trying to prevent teacher career stagnation by providing more opportunities for ESL teachers to grow as professionals throughout their careers. As noted above, however, all three ESL teachers said that they felt underappreciated by their administration and that the administration did not know exactly what ESL teachers in the school did either inside or outside their classrooms. All three teachers said that they usually performed extra extracurricular activities without any recognition or affirmation from the administration at all but that they did these because they wanted to help their students. Indeed, one teacher noted that the administration always seem to make decisions directly related to the ESL teachers in inopportune moments when the ESL department were really busy and they took this as a further indication that the administration did not have a real understanding of what they do or when they do it in that particular institution. T1 noted: "When they make administrative decisions, they tend to do it at times when we're our busiest."

Regarding workload issues, T3 noted that she was confused about whom she was working for when she was "asked" to do some other work, such as fund raising; she noted: "I was quite concerned about how I conducted my job. Before I was hired as a full time faculty I was partial load, do I did my work hours and then I could do whatever I wanted to do. Now anything extra, anything, whether it be what I do for [fund raising], that was for the College. I was working for the College basically. It wasn't, it wasn't my free choice, which I totally disagree." T2 pointed out that:

> It's crazy how much time [people] in the department spend typing up letters and filling in forms and all these things that, it's a waste of people's knowledge and skills. It's just a waste. It frustrates me because I think other people have administrative assistants who do just everything for them so that they can, you know come up with creative ideas and wonderful thoughts.

T3 commented on how the restrictions and rules put into place by the administration affected how ESL teachers have to balance their time and priorities. For example, she was told by the administration that her research is seen as her own interest, and therefore not part of her work hours; T3 noted: "If you're doing something out of your own interest, such as your own research, the administration said that that's different. So anything that I do, and every one of us [ESL teacher], we do it out of the goodness of our hearts." T3 said that regardless of what the administration wanted, she would continue with her own research for the good of her students as she pointed out: "I don't really care because I think this generation of teachers is starting to say I value the quality of your education and experience you give to your students. I want to give them the best experience possible and the collective agreement is too much. It's not right." So, it seems that all three teachers' were influenced more by intrinsic rewards they received from their students rather than by any extrinsic rewards from the administration. If institutions want help prevent "plateauing" and encourage their ESL teachers to perform better, they should find ways to boost their morale by recognizing and affirming (verbally or otherwise) their important role within the school. They could also try to create a culture of teacher reflection and inquiry within their institutions where they encourage their teachers to form teacher reflection groups to reflect on their work.

Another factor that likely lead to plateauing is longevity as a teacher: research in general education studies has noted that the longer a teacher is teaching at the same institution, the greater the likelihood the teacher will experience some form of plateauing (Milstein, 1990; Meister and Ahrens, 2011). Since all three teachers have been teaching together at the same institution for the past 15 years, this may have influenced their perception of reaching a plateau although only T3 used the actual word "plateau." T3 further noted that because she had been teaching ESL in the same institution for a "long time," she now felt it was "time to take stock of how I'm doing in the classroom for both me and my students." However, although the other two teachers did not specifically refer to the phenomenon of plateauing, most likely because they were not aware of this phenomenon, T1 realized that she had come to a stage/phase in her teaching career where she stated she felt "tired." T2 said that she realized that she wanted to "explore myself [professionally] properly." In fact, and as was pointed out earlier, this was the genesis of their teacher reflection group: that all three teachers had arrived at a position in mid-career where they felt the need to reflect on their work.

## Reflective questions

- What do you think are the main causes of teacher plateauing?
- Do you feel appreciated by your administration? Why or why not?
- What are your duties as an ESL teacher in your school?
- How do you define and view your intrinsic and extrinsic rewards as a teacher?

## Coping with and resisting plateauing

Although not cognizant of any literature on teacher plateauing, the teachers seemed to find different ways to cope with their perceived mid-career stagnation and thus maintain their commitment and enthusiasm for their work. These were collaborating with colleagues, enhancing their feelings of self-efficacy during the group discussions, and seeking out professional development opportunities to further develop themselves as teachers. For example, one way the teachers were able to cope with plateauing was by collaborating with their colleagues so that they could reduce their feelings of isolation. As T2 noted, "So often you are out on your island 'Oh my God! Here I am by myself. Am I the only one having this issue?'" An example of collegial interactions with their colleagues was when T1 talked about working with another ESL teacher in the same institution (but not a member of the teacher reflection group reported on in this chapter) about her struggles teaching the same level class and she realized that as a result of her discussions with this colleague, she began to see her colleague "in a whole new role" as a "critical friend"; she said that her colleague "clicked into almost a mentor mode because she had taught speaking so much more than I have recently and then she came up with these [teaching] ideas." This critical friendship made her realize the value of colleagues collaborating; she continued: "It just started to hit me that as we were taking that we could do more together than this; that's what you need between colleagues to get this kind of thing going." T1 said that as a result she has since begun to meet with other colleagues to discuss her teaching; she said: "I'm meeting with other teachers and we're talking about our teaching. We're trying to become better teachers. I like to share what I learn with them." T3 also reflected on her collaborations with other ELS teacher colleagues within the college and how she found such collaborations reassuring for her own teaching; she noted: "It was just one of those things where you always knew but it was kind of nice to see that people have some sort of common characteristics and you have to understand how each other is both working together as a staff."

Another way that the teachers were able to cope and tolerate frustrations related to their students' neediness and lack of mutuality was their strong sense of efficacy and their feelings of being able to make a difference. All three teachers noted during the group discussions that they carried out many extra extracurricular activities without any recognition or affirmation from the administration because they wanted to help their students. Indeed, these extracurricular activities may be unique to TESOL teachers are they help their students acculturate to not only a new language but also a new culture.

The teachers also reflected on their own development (or lack of development) as teachers in a type of stock taking reflective moment and the resulting need to seek out professional development opportunities (such as this teacher-initiated teacher reflection group). Of course, these reflections began at the establishment of the teacher-initiated reflection group when they all noted a need for some change in their professional lives. Apart from the **T1 realized** of this chapter, T2 realized that she needed to go out of her comfort zone and reflect on her development but that she was unsure of this too and hence her reason for joining the group to reflect on her work. T1 revisited her early reflections at the end of the project when she noted that she had reflected on most of her teaching life during that past semester; she remarked: "We are definitely moving out of our comfort zone there. If you want professional development as an ESL teacher, you need to revisit everything." T3 also suggested that she has grown as a teacher during the period of reflection because now instead of letting student problems get to her as she had in the past, now she does not let them bother her so much as she now realizes that learning is a student responsibility; she commented: "Now I feel like I'm sort of swaying the other way but I just keep saying to them, some of them will apologize 'I'm sorry I missed your test', and I want to say, 'I don't care. It's your learning, it's not mine'."

## Reflective questions

- What have you learned about teacher plateauing that you can use if you encounter it during your career?
- Why would developing strategies for dealing with plateauing be a good idea for all language teachers?
- How can you keep your interest levels up when teaching in the same institution for a long period?
- How can a teacher reflection group work for the good of the group while at the same time facilitating individual members' reflections?

Although all three teachers experienced some plateauing, not all experienced the same level of plateauing. For example, Milstein (1989) has pointed out that teachers can be considered to reach a level of either "high-plateauers" or "low-plateauers." "High-plateauers" tend to have negative feelings, and are more skeptical about their work as teachers, while "low-plateauers" tend to have more positive feelings, and are less skeptical about their work as teachers. While it may seem that at various times during the study reported on in this chapter, and especially at the initial stages of the group discussions in the teacher reflection group, that all three teachers may have exhibited some features and evidence of "high-plateauer" level, toward the end of the period of reflection the content of the topics discussed in the teacher reflection group suggest that all three exhibited more positive feelings toward their work and as such could be considered to have moved into a "low-plateauer" level. Indeed, the findings suggest that intensive discussions with colleagues in a teacher reflection group can help facilitate ESL teachers to make a move from the level of "high-plateauer" to the level of "low-plateauer." It is conceivable to say that the shared discourse in the group helped the teachers to articulate their reflections on teaching by making the tacit explicit because these teacher conceptions often remain hidden. If, as was pointed out above, that all teachers are susceptible to some kind of plateauing during their careers and especially in mid-career, then the question of how we can help teachers and administrators cope with plateauing becomes important.

## Setting up a teacher reflection group

The results of this reflection project suggest that ESL teachers may be able to resist plateauing if the engage in critical reflection in a teacher reflection group. Indeed as the next chapter also indicates, engaging in such critical reflection within such a group can lead to teacher expertise and overall career satisfaction. In this section I outline how teachers can set up a teacher reflection group based on the experiences of the teacher reflection group outlined in this book.

A teacher reflection group is a place for ESL teachers to come together to talk about their work in a supportive and evaluation free environment. When forming such groups teachers must consider many issues such as: the type of group they want, the number of participants to include at formation, the different roles of each participant, what to discuss, how to sustain the group, and how to evaluate the group once the reflection period has ended.

## Type of group

When considering the type of group that ESL teachers would want to reflect in, the overall philosophical approach to the group should be considered and discussed. For example, although never really articulated by the members, the overall philosophical approach to the group reported on in this book was one of *power-with* where collaboration was emphasized and members did not impose their interests, topics, or values on one another. Rather, they mutually fulfilled their desires by acting together as a group rather than individuals within a group. As Kriesberg (1992) has noted, a *power-with* type group empowers its members because members find ways to satisfy their desires and to fulfill their interests without imposing these on each other. Kriesberg (1992: 85–86) continues: "The relationships of co-agency is one in which there is equality: situations in which individuals and groups fulfill their desires by acing together. It is jointly developing capacity." T1 noted after the period of reflection that "It seemed to me that we wanted to find topics of mutual interest to pursue and discuss where the group could go forward together as one." The alternative type of group is *power-over* characterized by command and control (by members or a facilitator), but as Kriesberg (1992: 47) also notes, power-over relationships "cuts off human communication and creates barriers to human empathy and understanding." Therefore, all the members in the teacher reflection group must be willing to commit to the support of one another's reflective practices if it is to be an empowering experience for each member. Once this issue is discussed and agreed upon, the teacher reflection group can consider where they want to draw their members from and how many members they want in it.

Farrell (2007) has outlined three main types of teacher reflection groups and they can extend not only within the school but may span several schools or school districts as well as other organizations: *peer groups* can be set up within a school, *teacher groups* can be set up at the district level, *district level groups*, and virtual groups that can be formed anywhere. The teacher reflection group formation reported on in this chapter comes under peer groups (a group with their colleagues in the same institution), and as one participant suggested, the ideal number should be no more than four was "enough for a group because there was always the concern about one person dominating the conversation" (T1). Once a group of teachers decide that they want to form a teacher reflection group they must then figure out how they want to operate such a group in terms of general rules of the group, participants' roles, and topic setting. When deciding what type of group to form, teachers must be on aware of two different types of groups: power-with and power-over groups.

## Reflective questions

- What is your understanding of a *power-with* type group?
- What is your understanding of a *power-over* type group?
- What type of teacher reflection group (TRG) would you like to set up and why?
- How would you set it up?

### Forming the group

Richardson (1997) has suggested that when colleagues come together in a group to reflect on their work, four basic features or ingredients need to be present if the group is to be successful:

1. Each participant needs to feel "safe" within the group. In the teacher reflection group reported on in this book, T2 commented: "My colleagues are also my friends and I feel extremely comfortable sharing my thought with them."
2. Each participant needs to feel "connected" in some way or other. In the teacher reflection group reported on in this book, T3 commented: "The group provided time to share common experiences, ask for or offer insights and advice, and ponder solutions."
3. Each participant has to have a sense and to be able to feel passionate about the group and what they are trying to accomplish together. In the teacher reflection group reported on in this book, T1 later reflected: "Face to face discussion was important for bonding the group and renewing our commitment to the process each week."
4. Each participant must honor, and be grateful for the group's existence. In the teacher reflection group reported on in this book, T3 noted that: "It was nice to be able to affirm and support each other as we expressed concerns or doubts, too."

As can be seen from the teachers' comments, the above four features were important for defining the group's existence for the participants in the case study reported in this chapter because they sought out each other (and the facilitator) for the camaraderie of working together as a teacher reflection group. Thus, such teacher reflection groups should offer moral support where vulnerabilities shared and aired in a safe environment.

Risk taking should also be encouraged in such groups where self-confidence is enhanced by positive encouragement and feedback for each of the group members. That said, group members should not just validate everything each member says about their practice simply because a member said it. In fact, this was probably the biggest weakness of the teacher reflection group reported on in this book because the members tended to agree mostly with all the group comments and there was little challenging of other member's comments. As T1 noted after the period of reflection:

> I don't think we were especially critical of each other. We tended not to challenge or disagree. Our long-term professional relationship and friendship is too precious to risk. I think we tended to question or judge ourselves more harshly and then the other two would rush in to say—don't be so hard, or to support what the teacher had done However, we did give examples of how we do things differently and provided alternatives through anecdotal experiences of our own.

Teacher reflection groups must be on guard against overly romanticizing the teacher's voice; rather such groups should also be a place where constructive criticism and even conflict is welcomed because such critical dialogue can be a necessary catalyst for any change.

## Reflective questions

- How would you cover the four basic features for forming a group above?
- Why is risk taking important for a teacher reflection group?
- Why would conflict lead to change?
- Why should group members not just validate everything another member says in a group?
- Why should groups be on guard against overly romanticizing the teacher's voice?

### Group roles

Each teacher reflection group will be composed of members with different roles; one of the most important being the group's leader. Perhaps a democratic approach to discussions, where nobody attempts to manipulate the group into doing what he/she wants. It may also be possible for a teacher development group to have a type of coexisting leadership in order to provide more opportunities for getting the task done (one co-leader) and maintaining group cohesion (another co-leader). The group can also ask for the help of a facilitator, as was the case in the study reported on in this paper. During the group discussions the three teachers tended to take on roles although they were not conscious of these roles. For example, T1 took on the roles of *team worker* because she was always trying to cement the group together and the role of *implementer* as she was always there to see that things were completed. The other two teachers also took on these roles but to a lesser extent. T2 took on the role of *monitor* because she wanted to ensure that all opinions and options were considered. T3 took on the role of *listener* as she was the most silent of the three.

## Reflective questions

- Discuss each role above.
- What other roles do you think would be necessary in your group?

### Modes of reflection

Once the group has discussed and agreed on the allocation of different roles for the period of reflection, they should then consider what opportunities they will provide for reflection. For example, the teacher reflection group reported on in this book decided to use the group discussions to aid their reflections in combination with regular journal writing, and some classroom observations of each other's lessons. Each group will have to discuss and agree on the number of meetings they can commit to during the period of their reflection as well and when they will all write in their teacher journal and if and when they will observe each other teach. All members of the teacher reflection group seemed to like and benefit from the combination of talking, writing, and observing rather than focusing on any one of these modes of reflection. As T1 noted:

> I liked the cycle and interplay between the realities of my classroom and workplace, the journal, the discussion group and then small classroom research or PD activities. Any of them on their own would have been "ok" but together they really enriched the experience. It was a full experience. I got to study my classroom and students; reflect upon myself as a teacher (quite specifically and holistically); and feel supported by my colleagues and learn from them (including the facilitator).

Of course, other teacher reflection groups may want to consider other modes of reflection and adjust the three talked about above to their own particular setting and needs.

## Reflective questions

- What is your preference for a mode of reflection from talking, writing and/or observing?
- Which mode would be easiest for you and why?
- Which mode would be difficult for you and why?

### Discussion topics

When teacher reflection groups come together for the first time they may or may not have a focus for the group discussions. The group reported on in this paper did not have any particular topics in mind from the beginning, so they just let topics emerge and develop from their teaching and discussions at that time. In addition, the group did not have any other similar group to compare with nor did they have a list of topics they could consider. So, other groups may want to first brainstorm a theme or topic together and then narrow it down by identifying specific questions to explore. This narrowing down of a topic allows participants to focus their attention on issues that have personal meaning for them. The group can also at this stage decide if they have the resources available for them to continue reflecting on that particular topic. When the topic is temporarily exhausted, then the group can start another cycle of brainstorming a topic followed by a narrowing of the topic with development of specific questions addressing that topic. In the case study reported in this chapter the facilitator (this author) started each group discussion for the first few meetings but then the participants themselves began to set the topics for each meeting after that. Other groups could also consider the topics that emerged from the group reported in this paper to see if they are universal for experienced ESL teachers; the topics were in order of frequency: *school context, perceptions of self as teacher, learners,* and *approaches and methods in practice.*

## Reflective questions

- Would you discuss the topics mentioned above?
- What other topics would you want to discuss in your group?

### Sustaining the group

In order to sustain any teacher reflection group each member must be committed to the group. The teacher reflection group in the study reported on in this chapter lasted for one semester intensively and another semester intermittingly. For the first semester, the group met each Saturday morning for one or two hours to reflect on their work. Commitment for intensive reflection with a group of teachers should last ideally for one semester according to the teachers reported on in this paper. Although the beginning of this teacher reflection group was shaky in terms of commitment, when they all realized the benefits of the reflective process, they all made most of these meetings. As T2 noted in her postgroup reflections, "I admit that when we first talked about giving up Saturday morning I felt a bit concerned about whether I had made the right choice but in the end felt it was time well spent."

Because teaching is a very personal activity, as teachers in a reflection group begin to open up and discuss professional (and personal) issues that are important to them with other teachers whom they may or may not know, there will inevitably be a certain level of anxiety present. So a nonthreatening environment of trust should be fostered in the group. Although trust was not an issue in the group reported on in this chapter because the teachers were colleagues and friends for over 15 years, one teacher did mention it in her post group reflections: T1 talked about trust: "I think that establishing trust is the key factor in creating an environment that supports cooperative discussion and reflection." Ways of establishing trust can be incorporated into the reflective process itself, such as emphasizing description and observation over judgment in group discussions as was the case in the study reported on in this chapter.

## Reflective questions

- How can you plan for sustaining your group?
- Do you think having a set period for reflections will help sustain the group?
- How will you approach the issue of trust in the group?
- How can you establish group trust?

## Evaluating the group

After a teacher reflection group concludes its period of reflection it is important that all group participants evaluate the influences of the group on their personal and professional growth so that they can have some closure. Participants can reflect on whether they achieved their individual and group goals, their individual and the group accomplishments and factors that can be considered if they or others want to set up another teacher development group. As T1 reflected after the group experience:

> We shared what was happening in our classrooms and professional lives. I don't think we found solutions per say, but I think we provided a forum for each of us as individuals to articulate what was happening and then to share similar experiences in a supportive way

Also they can at this stage the group can consider if they want to share their findings with other teachers who may benefit from hearing about their experiences. They can attend a conference and report about their group to other teachers and they can also write up the group developments for a journal publication. The participants in the group reported on in this chapter presented their views at a later conference in which they summarized their participation in this teacher reflection group very favorably. T1 noted at the end of the reflective period: "I think this experience has given me the confidence, skills and motivation to continue this type of PD in the future and to enjoy my teaching in this new phase of my career that I feel is coming up."

## Reflective questions

• How will you evaluate the success of your group?
• How will you be able to evaluate the "cycle and interplay between the realities of my classroom and workplace, the journal, the discussion group and then small classroom research or PD activities"?

## Benefits of teacher reflection groups

From the results of the experiences of the teacher reflection group reported on in this book, I will end this chapter citing two of the most important benefits the teachers have received from participating in such a group with the hope that other language teacher professionals can obtain similar benefits.

### Promote collegial support

Language teacher reflection groups provide a forum for a group of teachers to encourage each other to examine their practice and receive positive feedback, emotional support, and empathy. As was noted earlier in the book, because teaching is often considered an isolated profession with teachers alone in a class behind a closed door for much of their careers, a more collegial type of reflection with a group of like-minded colleagues can help teacher overcome any feelings of isolation and produce a more collaborative mentality. Such collaborative interactions can also help reduce and alleviate (and possibly wipeout) teacher burnout associated with have reached a career plateau and increase morale and ultimately lead to more job satisfaction. Throughout the process of reflection in such a group the participants also learn how to build professional relationships so that they too can share their new found reflections with other teachers outside the group and act as mentors for other language teachers.

### Promote reflection on practice

Language teacher reflection groups can promote continuous reflective practice by encouraging teachers to be on guard against blindly following routine and by acting more deliberately about what they will teach, why they will teach it, when they will teach it, and what the impact of their teaching was. Thus teacher reflection groups can help teachers to become less guided by impulses or perceptions or intuitions and be guided more by reflection. In this way they can make more deliberate and informed decisions about their practice, thus taking responsibility for their classroom actions. Teachers can share their effective practices, and teaching materials and activities with members within the group and this can lead to overall improved teaching practices as they share ways of applying theory into classroom practices. This sharing can also be extended outside the group with colleagues within their own institutions, thus promoting more collegial exchanges in other institutions.

## Conclusion

This chapter summed up how language teachers can meet teacher plateauing head-on while reflecting in a teacher reflection group. The chapter outlined and discussed the various causes of plateauing from the three teachers' perspective such as the front-loaded nature of teaching, the administration's role regarding workload issues, and teacher longevity. The chapter also discussed how teachers can cope and resist plateauing from the examples provided by the teachers such as collaborating with colleagues, enhancing their feelings of self-efficacy during the group discussions, and seeking out professional development opportunities to further develop themselves as teachers. The chapter also outlined in detail how teachers can set up a teacher reflection group similar to the one presented in this book. For example, after deciding on what type of group they want to form, group members must then decide the different roles they will take on, their preferred modes of reflection, what topics they want to discuss, how they will sustain the group, and also how they will evaluate the success of the group.

# 9
# Developing Teacher Expertise

## Introduction

What is an expert? Many will likely answer that it is a person in any field who performs his or her job in a seemingly effortless manner so much so that it looks automatic and comes from all the years of experience performing this particular job. In the field of education some teachers have been regarded as experts only because of their years of experience in a classroom, but as Tsui (2003) has noted, the number of years of teaching experience does not necessarily translate into expertise. Indeed Woods (1996) has cautioned although "one teacher may have had ten years of experience, another may have had one year's experience ten times" (Woods, 1996: 270). Within the field of TESOL teacher expertise is still a very under-researched topic (Rodríguez and McKay, 2010). This final chapter then explores all the data presented so far in relation to teacher expertise. I first looked at the literature on teacher expertise and then scanned all the data in an attempt to outline specific characteristics of ESL teacher expertise exhibited by the three teachers. First I discuss what teacher expertise is, then outline the specific characteristics of teacher expertise found in the data, and finally recommend how ESL teachers in mid-career can seek to become expert ESL teachers.

## Teacher expertise

In order to address the topic of teacher expertise it is important to first consider what "experience" means and if experience translates into expertise making a person an "expert." Experience obviously comes from doing something for some time over a person's career life cycle. As we have already seen in the Huberman (1989) model of teacher life cycles there are three main phases in teachers' life cycles: novice, mid-career, and late-career. In this Huberman (1989) model teacher expertise has been equated with years of teaching, and this has been used by educational administrations and school boards as an indication of achieving some sort of expertise along the way from this experience through classroom teaching and other education duties. Some administrators have also used student achievement on test scores but the whole idea of experience leading to expertise has been questioned by various researchers (e.g. Bereiter and Scardamalia, 1993; Johnson, 2003, 2005; Tsui, 2003, 2005, 2009). Indeed, Tsui (2003: 194) has suggested that some teachers can only be considered as "experienced non-experts" because they "rely more on routines as they become more experienced and solve problems at a superficial level." It is important then to consider what an "expert" is.

Johnson (2003, 2005) suggests that expertise has something to do with knowledge, but not "just a headful of facts" (Bereiter and Scardamalia, 1993: 30) about a particular topic. As Johnson (2005: 13) suggested, it "is the quality of knowledge that is important" in terms of possessing the "'judgment of promisingness' [where] the expert knows which avenues are likely to be promising and which may turn out to be dead ends." An expert, as Johnson (2005) points out, does not always go about his or her work in a very logical, thorough or systematic way. Indeed, Johnson (2005: 15) suggests when novice-expert studies are compared the findings will likely highlight the effortless performance on the part of experts because of their knowledge: "Those who have knowledge do not need to think so much, while those lacking the knowledge base are forced into the harder route." However, Johnson (2005: 15–16) and others caution that "the apparent ease of experts often belies immense effort" because they "work long hours ... and they tend to set standards for themselves and others that are always at least slightly beyond reach."

Tsui (2009) maintains that expertise includes a person's ways of knowing, acting, and being of experts in a particular domain. Similar to other fields, much of the early studies on teacher expertise compared novice and expert teachers and what they do and think in the classroom. Tsui (2005, 2009) has noted two main characterizations of teaching expertise: expertise as a "state" and as a "process." Expertise as a state looks as characteristics associated with a teacher after years of teaching experiences whereas expertise as a process examined teachers' development of different characteristics over time. Both of these approaches have, as Tsui (2005) has observed, produced different characterizations of teaching expertise.

Tsui (2009) identified characteristics of expert teachers during different phases of classroom teaching: pre- and post-active phases and interactive phase. In the pre- and post-active phases she noted that expert teachers always start their lesson planning with their knowledge of the students not only as groups but also as individual learners. They are able to exercise autonomy in decision making, they respond flexibly to contextual variations such as student responses, disruptions, and available resources, they are more efficient in lesson planning, and their lesson plans are usually brief. In addition, she noted that expert teachers' planning thoughts show a much more integrated knowledge base and they are able to relate their lessons to the entire curriculum and to other curricula and to establish coherence between lessons. During the interactive phase of teaching, experts are characterized according to Tsui (2009: 192) by how they deal with the complexities of classroom teaching, "Which are typified by multidimensionality, simultaneity, immediacy, and unpredictability of classroom events." As such, because of their experience as teachers, experts are able to recognize patterns in classroom events interpret these patterns in meaningful ways. They are also more selective about what they attend to in the classroom, have better improvisational skills and can draw on a repertoire of routines with automaticity and effortlessness. One other are that teachers are expert teachers is in how they interpret classroom events by providing a deeper analysis of problems, as they "justify their practices in a principled manner" (Tsui, 2009: 193).

## Reflective questions

- What is an expert?
- Do you know any experts? If yes, please identify some of the characteristics that make that person an expert.
- What is an expert teacher to you?
- Do you think expertise is a *state* or a *process*? Explain your answer.
- Does experience always translate into expertise?
- Do you consider yourself an expert? Why or why not?

## Teachers' characteristics of expertise

Globally, the five main characteristics of teacher expertise that were manifested in the group discussions, interviews and teaching journals were (in order of frequency): *Knowledge of Learners and Learning, Engage in Critical Reflection, Access Past Experiences, Informed Lesson Planning,* and *Active Student Involvement.*

## Knowledge of learners and learning

The first characteristic that the teachers exhibited in their group discussions, interviews, and teacher journals was their knowledge of their learners and learning. This is a similar finding as Richards (1998) and Richards, Li, and Tang (1998) when they noted that expert teachers show a deeper understanding of students and language learning (Richards, 1998; Richards et al., 1998). This characteristic of teacher expertise included such topics as how the three teachers were sensitive to their students' needs, moods, motivation, enjoyment, learning styles, and also how they attempted to build relationships and rapport with their students but also how they made sure their students realized that they were responsible for their own learning. One dilemma within learners and learning characteristic the teachers had to show their expertise was how to balance keeping students happy because they are considered "clients" by their institution versus pushing them to work hard and do things they need to do to learn the language. For example, T2 said that she felt the pressure to pass students because of school financial reasons and that this feeling triggered bad memories from past schools she worked in that had similar reasons for retaining students: T2 continued:

> I feel more so now than when we first started there that the pressure on retention and keeping the customers happy has triggered all those past feelings that we've all been there, we've all worked in those schools: "we've got to keep the customers happy. We've got to keep them paying their money and that kind of thing."

For T2 this issue required her to use all her experience as a teacher to try to find a balance between trying to keep students happy while at the same time getting them to do the things they need to learn the second language. As T2 said: "I think there is a big conflict between keeping people happy and helping them to learn what they need. I think you need to balance them." T1 agreed and said: "You definitely need to balance those two things because you can teach them what they need to know but they may not enjoy it. If they don't enjoy it they will go somewhere and learn what they need to know in a place that they do enjoy it." T3 also agreed and commented that as experienced ESL teachers they have to be realistic and understand that their students are clients as in a business; she continued: "I think they can be both. You can also have learners who are clients and you can provide them with the service that you are supposed to be providing them with and still be an educator."

Then T2 cautioned that it is not easy to balance this idea of students as customers because as she commented: "You can also start to believe that everything that the students want is the right thing and that's the danger." T3 agreed and suggested: "The customer is always right? No. I don't go for that." However, all three realize that the administration may have a different idea for paying ESL students. As T1 noted:

Then it affects your whole school because if administration sees the numbers and the dollars and that becomes more important than the learning, not to say that happens with us because I don't think it does. But you have to be constantly aware of it because it is easy to go that way.

Indeed, T3 suggested that even though they might have to retain students for the schools' financial reasons it will not help the student learn English and so they noted the ESL teacher must try to find some balance here; as T3 noted: "Ultimately that doesn't serve them well. They aren't learning for the sake of learning. It's a balance of learning English and qualifications which is fine. You can have both. You can learn English and get a piece of paper."

Embedded in this topic is another balancing act of trying to teach their students English while also trying to retain them given their institution's pressure stated above. They noted that that their classroom tasks, topics, and activities must be structured with both in mind: teaching and entertaining students for retention purposes, but that finding a balance between both is difficult as T2 noted when she said: "I really wonder if the classroom tasks, topics, and activities I perceive to be entertaining or enjoyable are actually enjoyable to my learners." T1 wondered about the value of entertaining: "What is the value of the entertainment factor? What is the value of the actual learning? And how do the two go together in my classes?" So T1 said that achieved such a balance by giving her students choices about what topics they were interested in at the beginning of the semester; she said: "Some people like to read science and some don't so I have them at the beginning do a survey of their interests so when I'm planning I can incorporate them." However, she said that she does not necessarily cover all their topics during the semester because she noted that she obviously cannot cover 30 (the number of students in her class) different topics in a 15 week semester but also because she will choose some topics they may have omitted that she thinks necessary they cover. The important point here is that this teacher informs her students what she is going to do in her reading classes and why by taking them through the process: "I just make them aware of the process that I go through" and then as she says she will not have to listen to comments later in the course if they feel bored about a particular topics: "I don't want to deal with it later where they are all 'I'm bored of this topic. I don't like this topic'."

Related to the issue of their perceptions of the level of interest their students had in their lessons was how they achieve some sort of balance with students who frustrate them during lessons by not paying attention and how they can motivate them to keep on track to learn English. For example, T2 mentioned that she gets frustrated with students who do not try to complete their homework or help other students learn. She said: "I'm frustrated because it interferes with what I'm trying to accomplish with the rest of the class." They all noted that even though they will try to help their students learn that ultimately it is their responsibility as T1 noted: "I know that if the students are responsible for their learning, I'll do my best with the knowledge I have to make it possible, make the environment possible for them but ultimately if they don't want to, that's fine." T3 also made a similar comment and took an even strong position that students are responsible for their own learning; she said: "When students don't help themselves, it is especially disappointing to you. Oh well, they are adults. I don't care. I mean, I'll also help but ultimately it is up to the student to learn."

## Reflective questions

- What is it about the characteristic *knowledge of learners and learning* that would make it necessary for expertise?
- What does the characteristic *knowledge of learners and learning* mean to you?
- What do you think the teachers did above to signify that they have in fact such a characteristic from what was reported?
- Is there anything else that you think should be considered a part of this characteristic?

### Engage in critical reflection

The next most frequent expert characteristic was how they all engaged in some form of critical reflection and critical examination of their own practices. Included in these reflections is their stated desire to further investigate a wide range of teaching issues they are interested in. Some of this interest arose from their current reflections on practice within the teacher reflection group reported on in this chapter, and some from their reflections gained from attending conferences. This is also a similar finding to Tsui (2003) in that all three teachers were seeking some sort of continuous renewal by critically reflecting on their practices.

All three teachers said that they realized that critical examination is a very important part of being an experienced ESL teacher. They suggested that it is valuable because it allows them to examine their "methods, techniques, tricks, relationships with students, and how their job fits into their lives" (comment by T1). T2 mentioned that she felt the continuous need to examine her teaching because she felt it has become too automatic for her over the years and as a result she wondered if she really understood what she was doing; she reflected:

> Am I "Reading" my students correctly? Has this process become so automatic, so sub-conscious, and so intuitive that I don't know? Do I rely on my experience too much when making decisions? Maybe I should be making this process more conscious for both myself and my students.

Another reason they said that they wanted to critically examine their practice was that they wanted to be able to compare different methods of teaching so that as T3 noted, "they could better control their decisions about which method would provide better learning opportunities for their students." One such method they discussed was trying to get their students' input and feedback to help them solve problems in their classrooms. The teachers said that they felt that discussing issues with their students and asking for their ideas and suggestions is a good method to resolve any problems in the classroom such as which method works or does not work, whether students enjoy a certain activity, or participate in activities. With this approach of including their students in their reflections and decision making, the teachers found that students gained a sense of responsibility to their own learning when being asked for their input and ideas. T3 relayed an example of this:

> Yesterday I sat down with my class as I had 20 minutes of class left and I said: "Okay, how much do you enjoy class?" So I put them in groups and I asked them, how important is it to you to have enjoyment in your class? And then what kind of things that are done in class is valued? It was sort of this even balance of "well, if I'm not enjoying it it's boring" and I said, "Wait a minute, is the opposite of boring enjoyment or interesting?" They went "Oh!" They stopped and looked at me.

T2 also agreed it is a good idea to include their students and to encourage them to reflect on their own learning; she said: "It's good for them to explore it themselves and to reflect." Her example of this occurred in one class when she asked her students to comment about their preference for pair work or group work. T2 continued: "I said, do you want to work in pairs, or groups of three, or groups of four and I let them choose." When they had chosen T2 then asked them to reflect on their choices: "At the end, I asked them. Why didn't you want to work in pairs? Why did you choose threes? We just talked about it. I don't think I would have done that before. I would have just said, I've decided we're going to work in a pair."

The teachers also all agreed that professional development sessions, discussions with others, and collaboration with other teachers are all great ways to reflect on their practice because they help find solutions to problems they might be having. T1 noted: "I'm very interested in how teachers can help each other. I see great potential for team building and collaboration coming out of something like this." T1 continued to recount how she and another teacher collaborated on how to teach a reading class that semester and how they set this collaboration up; T1 remarked:

> We are both teaching reading so we are going to choose some material that would be appropriate for both Level 3 and Level 4 and then teach a lesson with it. We are not going to tell the other what we are going to do with the material and then observe each other to see what we did. Just for fun and curiosity.

The teachers said that they really appreciated collaboration and felt that it is something that should be done often because it can help minimize one's workload and helps teachers be consistent in terms of grades and what students across all sections are being taught. In all, the teachers felt that collaboration with peers is like having small professional development sessions and helps them add variety in their lessons.

## Reflective questions

- What is it about the characteristic *engage in critical reflection* that would make it necessary for expertise?
- What does the characteristic *engage in critical reflection* mean to you?
- What do you think the teachers did above to signify that they have in fact such a characteristic from what was reported?

- Is there anything else that you think should be considered a part of this characteristic?

## Assess past experiences

The next most frequent expert characteristic was their ability to access and make use of their past experiences. In studies on the development of expertise Ericsson and Smith (1991: 30) have noted that "access to aggregated past experience is the single most important factor accounting for the development of expertise." Although the third most important factor in frequency accounting for the three teachers' expertise in this study, it was very important because the teachers showed their knowledge of the different trends and cycles of their classrooms, and themselves as ESL teachers in general. They indicated that they possess the ability to make intuitive judgments based on their combined past experiences, and the ability to integrate knowledge from a wide range of sources such as professional journals, conferences, and their colleagues' comments. In addition, they all seem to have a wide repertoire of routines and strategies from past experiences from which to call upon.

T1 and T2 noted that they tended to teach to a pattern in their own classes that follows the cycle of the semester; as T1 noted: "I think the teaching term does go in a cycle for teachers and students" and this happened at the beginning of the second semester when T2 noted, "I'm at the beginning of the cycle that I described last term." All three teachers then reflected on the pattern they observed where they moved from being a "nice teacher" to being "strict teacher" and this usually occurred after the mid-term exams. T1 reflected that she noticed that in all their classes that the students' attitudes had changed after the mid-terms in any given semester and so had the teachers' way of teaching; she said:

> We all noticed last week that after midterm exams the students were getting tired. Students haven't done the homework in W's class this week and they didn't do the homework last week and this week for me either. They're absent more or coming late. T2's cracking the whip, and T3's having hissy fits.

T2 also noted the change in her attitude towards her students after the mid-term period each semester and that this usually happens if her students do not do what she wants them to do; T2 observed: "We all seem to have similar issues with our groups of students that we tried so hard to love and motivate before the exams and now we're all coming down on them. I thought that was very interesting and also a very familiar pattern. I think it often happens that way." T3 agreed and suggested that this trend happens every term; T3 continued: "it happens all the time. It's not just this term. It's the same pattern every time. Sometimes it starts earlier and right away you notice it."

All three teachers also seem to possess the ability to make intuitive judgments about their practice based on past experiences and are comfortable with these decisions as T3 noted: "I think it's perfectly fine to rely on your experience." T3 then explained that it is not just blindly following these past experiences but doing so in a professional manner; T3 continued:

> You would rely on it [past experience] in a professional way, not just to say "I've always done this. It's always been that way. This is my experience. I know this pattern is the same all the time therefore I don't have to change." I think you know as a professional, from your experience the things that worked and not worked and why they haven't happened.

T3 and T2 noted that this was not always the case with some of their colleagues even though they may have years of teaching experience. For example, T2 talked about one of her senior colleagues (who since retired) always followed the book, "page-by-page and she delivered the same thing all the time, for years, no change." T3 then remarked from her conversations observations of both T2's and T1's classes during the period of reflection reported on in this study, she knows that both do not do the same thing each semester or each year; as T3 observed: "I know that you do not follow routine. I know that you are focused on your students. You know what needs to be done but you present it to them in a way as adult learners that they can manage it to make it their own experiences." T1 then stated that they also make teaching decisions based on their accumulated experiences of how to "read their students' reactions" in class when she suggested that they look for clues from their students' reactions. T1 noted:

> We use all our experience to observe their behaviour in class, their facial expressions, and body language and we try to judge if learning has taken place. Sometimes, but rarely, we get direct verbal feedback. More often than not it is those subtle clues that we pick up as we make our way through our class: the little signs, or not so little, that let you know that something is "working" or "not working" and then the decision about what to do next.

The teachers then revealed that they have a wide repertoire of routines and strategies they can call upon when making instructional decisions as T1 noted: "there is no one method that we know that works every time but you want to make sure that whatever you're doing that your students are engaged in it." She then said that she uses both her "experience teaching as well as some old stand-bys in my filing cabinet." She continued: "My stand-bys are my 'bag of tricks' that consists of all the ideas, lessons, strategies, approaches, techniques, even jokes that have worked, and didn't work, over the last 15 years." However, rather than use these haphazardly she remarked that she uses them "in a principled manner"; she continued:

> I don't use them all the time with every group of students or with every course I teach. I select them carefully and pull them out when I think it is appropriate. Yes, I have my own philosophy to teaching (however conscious or subconscious it may be) but this is reflected more concretely in my day to day choices, my practices, and preferences in teaching. I am not an indiscriminate user of tricks in the classroom.

T2 said that she makes use of her repertoire of routines according to her students' needs and her own preference as a teacher. T2 stated:

> We all try different things according to what we know of our students, our own personalities and preferences, and what has worked in the past to motivate and engage our students in learning. That is choosing topics/tasks that we hope they like, creating an appropriate environment. These approaches and strategies have evolved over time and have been retried and refined in various teaching contexts.

## Reflective questions

- What is it about the characteristic *access past experiences* that would make it necessary for expertise?
- What does the characteristic *access past experiences* mean to you?
- What do you think the teachers did above to signify that they have in fact such a characteristic from what was reported?
- Is there anything else that you think should be considered a part of this characteristic?

## Informed lesson planning

The next most frequent expert characteristic was exhibited through their informed lesson planning, a similar characteristic of teacher expertise discussed by Tsui (2005, 2009). Lesson planning in this study included such lesson planning attributes as planning with efficiency, with comfort, with ease; ability to anticipate events of a lesson; strategies for focusing on lesson planning; not dependent on the original lesson plan if the lesson takes them in a different direction and to accommodate their students' needs, challenges, and interests. This expertise characteristic also included incorporating student responses into their lesson planning.

The teachers said that they believed that over-planning their lessons is not good and that sometimes they noted that lessons that are not planned out carefully or detailed can "end up being better lessons than very structured, rigid, lessons" (T2 comment). T1 noted that she tries to find some balance between focusing on content to be delivered and bringing her personality into a lesson when she plans. For this she has decided that less planning is best because the lesson tends to go smoother for her. T1 commented: "I have to find my own time that I relate to my students during the less, some kind of balance between content and being myself. I find that, you know how when you don't prepare too much things go better." T2 agrees and reflected that some of her best classes were not well prepared beforehand; T2 remarked:

> Sometimes my best classes are the ones I have not spent much time planning for. Funny how that goes! Of course, this is not always the case. I think, in my case, the fact that I have taught reading numerous times might have something to do with my success despite a lack of careful planning.

They also reflected on the notion that over the years, their views toward lesson planning have changed. They spend less time on planning now compared to when they started off because they all came to a realization that it's not worth spending copious amounts of time planning a lesson as the actual execution of a lesson is more often than not different from what they originally intended it to be. T3 reflected this opinion when she said: "I certainly don't plan my lessons the same way that I used to at the beginning of it all, of course." Though they still find lesson planning to be time-consuming, frustrating, and unfruitful sometimes, they do enjoy lesson planning and feel personal satisfaction when good planning comes to fruition in the classroom. Again it comes to the issue of balance and T2 reflected this when she said:

> It's just that balance and if that's how much time I have, that's how much time I have. I leave the ESL classes often not a hundred percent

feeling, not content with what went on, feeling that there were other things that I could have done if I just had some more time I could have done this or I could have done that and it would have been so much better. I write it down and I say, next term I am going to do that.

When planning lessons, the teachers said that they always consider their students' needs, interests, abilities, and the levels of difficulty of the materials and take all these factors into consideration when designing lessons and that they are not afraid to change the lessons if they don't go according to plan. For example, T2 noted that although she tried to carefully plan one particular lesson on a cultural issue she thought was very close to her students' interests, she was nevertheless disappointed that it had not gone according to plan. T2 reflected:

I worked really hard (too hard) last Thursday prepping a lesson on Chinese New Year and Chinese Zodiac signs for my class. I feel this was timely. It was a well-organized and planned lesson in my humble opinion and level appropriate but it just did not go as I had imagined. Some people were not challenged enough while others seemed to struggle with simple vocabulary and getting through the text.

Because of this particular lesson she said that she decided to survey her students' interests before each lessons to see what would be appropriate for all her learners "and will use this for planning."

## Reflective questions

- What is it about the characteristic *informed lesson planning* that would make it necessary for expertise?
- What does the characteristic *informed lesson planning* mean to you?
- What do you think the teachers did above to signify that they have in fact such a characteristic from what was reported?
- Is there anything else that you think should be considered a part of this characteristic?

### Active student involvement

The fifth most frequent expert characteristic was active student involvement. Active student involvement in terms of teacher expertise included the teachers' positive views of keeping involved with their students outside of class. They called this "socializing" and they all noted socializing benefited their students' development and helped to prevent any problems their students would encounter because of moving to another country and the cultural adaptation issues associated with this. T2 remarked that she socializes with her students willingly: "It's a voluntary thing. You choose to do it because you want to form a relationship with your students over a period of time." In agreement T1 remarked: "Helping the students outside of class is not in the job description. It's not part of the job really. Nobody asks us to do it. It's something you do because you like your students."

They noted that they are happy to have more opportunities to get to know their students better because they genuinely care about and for their students' well-being. For example, T2 said that part of their professional practice as ESL teachers goes beyond classroom teaching: "it goes beyond the classroom, our relationships. It's part of creating a whole environment for them and building a community for them." T2 continued to comment on the importance of such a community for international students in order to help them acculturate better into a new country: "It is a part of building community and making them feel comfortable and help them acculturate better."

### Reflective questions

- What is it about the characteristic *active student involvement* that would make it necessary for expertise?
- What does the characteristic *active student involvement* mean to you?
- What do you think the teachers did above to signify that they have in fact such a characteristic from what was reported?
- Is there anything else that you think should be considered a part of this characteristic?

### Developing teacher expertise

The five main characteristics of teacher expertise outlined above are not isolated as each is linked to the other and each builds on the other. The teachers are knowledgeable of their learners and learning, they critically examine their own teaching, teaching materials, knowledge received regarding teaching, and access their accumulated past experiences, and they value, understand, and participate in collaborative relationships with colleagues to make informed decisions about lesson planning and lesson delivery. They also participate in, and value, socialization of and with their students by attending to extracurricular activities and student acculturation. However, if one word could summarize these experienced teachers' thoughts and feelings about their experiences and actions as outlined above it would be *balance*. This word came up in all five characteristics of teacher expertise and as such it is an important implication for the professional development to of experienced teachers and an important finding to add to the literature on ESL teacher expertise.

In order to achieve such balance the teachers agreed that it is necessary for a language instructor to take a step back and find a balance between doing their job the way it is expected to be done and trying to meet everyone's needs. T2 said: "Again it's all about balance. No, you can't just come in and do your stuff and leave." T3 summed up what they constantly strive to balance in their practice: "It's balancing what I want you to learn or what I think you need to learn or that you expressed a need to learn." This suggests that the concept of teacher expertise is always in flux as teachers attempt to find balance with dilemmas related to their practice. In other words, the finding from this study suggests that teaching expertise seems to be a *process* rather than a *state* and that one is always *becoming* and continuously evolving (Tsui, 2005, 2009). That said, I would suggest that it the process whereby teachers are constantly attempting to find balance in their work most likely leads to the *development* of ESL teacher expertise. This has implications for teacher development in that teacher educators can encourage ESL teachers to engage is particular actions that can lead to the development of their teacher expertise. These actions include getting ESL teachers to constantly update their subject and pedagogical knowledge, engage in critical reflection, and collaborate with colleagues to discover new information about teaching, access and critically examine past experiences, lesson planning, and outside class involvement with students so that they can push themselves to "edge of their competence" (Bereiter and Scardamalia, 1993: i).

The findings also suggest that conscious deliberations in the teacher reflection group, such as the one reported on in this book, which involving group discussions and/or journal writing may also have an important role to play in helping teachers develop their teacher expertise because such teacher reflection groups can provide a forum whereby experienced teachers can make explicit the tacit knowledge that they have gained from all their years of teaching experience. In other words, engaging in systematic reflections on practice allows teachers to theorize their practical knowledge so that they can develop personal interpretations of this knowledge in their specific contexts. One of the distinguishing features of the teachers reported on in this chapter is that all three teachers actively sought ways to reflect on their practice and as Tsui (2009: 190) points out: "It is the resistance to automaticity and continuous learning that distinguish the expert from the non-expert." Consequently, the findings suggest that teaching experience does not automatically translate into teacher expertise unless teachers consciously and actively reflect on these experiences and engage in deep explorations of their practices at various times throughout their careers as ESL teachers.

## Reflective questions

- Which of the five characteristics of teacher expertise outlined above do you possess?
- Which of the five do you think you would like to possess and why?
- What other characteristics of teacher expertise do you think are necessary for an ESL teacher?
- Do you push yourself to the edge of your competence as a teacher?
- How can you seek balance in your life as an ESL teacher?
- Do you think you can ever "arrive" to the position of expert?
- If yes, how will you know?
- If not, why not?
- After reading the contents of this book do you think you will try to seek out other teachers to form a similar teacher reflection group as the one reported on in this book?

## Conclusion

This chapter presented all the data once more in terms of teacher expertise. All three teachers exhibited various characteristics of expertise. The five main characteristics of teacher expertise identified were: Knowledge of Learners and Learning, Engage in Critical Reflection, Access Past Experiences, Informed Lesson Planning, and Active Student Involvement. In addition the teachers are constantly attempting to achieve a *balance* within and among the five main characteristics of teacher. It seems that teacher expertise is a process of becoming rather than reaching a state and that experience itself does not automatically translate into expertise. The three teachers presented in this book are not only expert ESL teachers but also caring professionals and a credit to the ELT profession.

# Final Reflections: Professional Self-Development

Most of the research on professional development in the field of language teacher has dealt with pre-service or in-service institutionalized programs. Also, most of these professional development programs involve some kind of intervention in the form of workshops, lectures, readings, demonstrations, and seminars; usually with some tangible reward at the end (a degree, a promotion, more money, or all three). Additionally, this type of intervention is usually carried out by so-called experts in the field with the idea that the content of the courses will be transferred to the teachers' classroom teaching. However, Freeman (1994) has questioned the transferability of this intervention as being not at all clear. Freeman (1994: 8–10) thus takes an interpretive view of teaching where "teachers are constantly involved in interpreting their worlds ... where teaching is a social practice, and where one cannot learn about it; one must learn through it." Freeman (1992: 16) has called for a different approach to teacher development in which teacher educators must radically rethink their own pedagogy: "We need to act less like our colleagues who are esteemed in universities and more like our colleagues who are effective in schools."

While there has been some indication of this effort to collaborate with practicing teachers in the field, most of this work originates in the university or by the experts, not by the teachers themselves. So, I suggest that experienced ESL/EFL teachers who come together to dialogue about their work (even if this dialogue is with the self) be recognized as a separate but equally important part of professional development in language teaching. This view of development can and should be supported by teacher educators and administrators as these teachers may find it difficult to pursue the process alone. For the most part, these groups of teachers do not seek any reward except for professional development, but they do need encouragement, support, and some feedback. This support and feedback could come in many forms such as participation in the form of providing materials for discussion providing a place for discussion, and providing feedback to the group.

If this approach to teacher development is different than institution-alized courses then what terminology would be appropriate to describe it, the second question posed above? Different terms have been used in the past by different advocates of different types of development. The three main terms in the literature are teacher training, teacher educa-tion, and teacher development. However, I suggest the term "profes-sional self-development" be used in the future to describe the process of individual ESL/EFL teachers coming together, in pairs or groups, to reflect on their work. This is not a neutral term, and it should not be used as a footnote in the professional literature. It provides for the fact that these teachers are not struggling with any complex problems in their work, nor do they seek any qualification; what they do seek is a self-initiated understanding of themselves as teachers of a complex subject in a complex environment.

Incorporated in this definition of professional self-development is the important component of reflection. I agree with Lange (1990: 249–250) who sees an intimate relationship between teacher reflection and teacher development. He says:

> The reflective process allows developing teachers' latitude to experi-ment within a framework of growing knowledge and experience. It gives them the opportunity to examine their relations with students, their values, their abilities, and their successes and failures in a real-istic context. It begins the developing teacher's path toward becoming an "expert teacher."

The small sample size of three experienced ESL teachers was intended to allow for careful examination of how a language teacher reflection group can support other experienced ESL teachers who want to reflect on their work. Indeed, this author is well aware that the results may not provide the basis for prescription for all experienced language teachers wishing to engage in reflective practice in a teacher reflection group because it was specific to a small group of three experienced ESL teachers in a specific context. However, it is my firm belief that much of what is described and discussed in this book will have relevance for all language teachers, teacher educators, and administrators regardless of their context. I hope that experienced language teachers who decided to join such a teacher reflection group have a positive experience while at the same time have some fun reflecting with their colleagues.

It was my honor and my privilege to introduce readers to these teachers and give a glimpse into the everyday realities that experienced ESL teachers are faced with in the hope that more experienced teachers will reflect on their practices and share these reflections with other teachers, teacher educators, and administrators so that we can begin to appreciate the wonderful work ESL and all foreign language teachers are doing the world over. Any errors of mistakes or interpretations or misinterpretations or even mistaken misrepresentations of these wonderful three teachers are entirely of my making and I apologize in advance if this is the case. I have attempted to present a true picture of what these teachers have experienced and I must say on reflection that these teachers are amazing professionals.

I will end this book by giving these wonderful teachers the last word. Although there sometimes might be negativity attached to PD and feelings might be hurt at first, the expert teachers believe that PD (one form being their group meetings) is extremely empowering. They also realized that it is often neglected even though it is very necessary. T1 reflected:

> I wondered what would be the result of this group and genuinely had no idea. Although we are not quite finished, I suspect at this point that the benefits have been to slow down from the hectic pace of teaching and co-ordinating and to restore a healthy balance to my career and life, to process some of the things that I have learned from both my education and my experience and to look at them more carefully, to develop a closer connection with my two best friends and colleagues and to establish a process or a dialogue that genuinely supports me in my work. I also feel I have established some degree of control.

All three teachers said that they felt that while writing, they had a heightened sense of awareness of what they do every day and gave them clarity to see their successes and failures in and out of the classroom. T2 reflected:

> I tend to be a thoughtful person generally but certainly journaling and talking to all has heightened my awareness of my own reflective and decision-making processes. It was a moment in the week when I am forced to sit down and think about myself and my workplace in a clear and coherent fashion.

T3 reflected:

> Finally, I hope that I can help to get other people in our department going on Reflective Practice. We all stand to benefit immensely, professionally of course, but also in our relationships with each other. The fact that we're all going to be in the same department for quite a few years means to me that something like this is quite important.

# References

Argyris, C. and Schön, D. 1974. *Theory in Practice: Increasing Professional Effectiveness*. San Francisco: Jossey-Bass.

Bailey, K., Bergthold, B., Braunstein, B., Fleischman, N., Holbrook, M., Tuman, J., Waissbluth, X. and Zambo, L. 1996. The Language Learner's Autobiography: Examining the "Apprenticeship of Observation." In D. Freeman and J. Richards (eds), *Teacher Learning in Language Teaching*. Cambridge: Cambridge University Press, 11–29.

Beijard, D., Meijer, P. C., and Verloop, N. 2004. Reconsidering Research on Teachers' Professional Identity. *Teaching and Teacher Education*, 20, 107–128.

Bell, B. and Gilbert, J. 1994. Teacher Development as Professional, Personal, and Social Development. *Teaching and Teacher Education*, 10, 483–497.

Bogdan, R. C. and Biklen, S. K. 1982. *Qualitative Research for Education: An Introduction to Theory and Methods*. Boston: Allyn and Bacon.

Boud, D. Keogh, R. Walker, D. 1985. *Reflection: Turning Experience into Learning*. London: Kogan Page.

Bereiter, C. and Scardamalia, M. 1993. *Surpassing Ourselves: An Inquiry into the Nature and Implications of Expertise*. Chicago: Open Court.

Brookfield, S. 1995. *Becoming a Critically Reflective Teacher*. San Francisco, CA: Jossey Bass

Bullough, R. V. 1997. Practicing Theory and Theorizing Practice in Teacher Education. In J. Loughran and T. Russell (eds). *Teaching about Teaching: Purpose, Passion and Pedagogy in Teacher Education*. London UK: Falmer Press, 13–31.

Burden, P. R. 1990. Teacher development. In Houston, R. W. (ed.), *Handbook of Research on Teacher Education*. New York: Macmillan, 311–328.

Burns, A. and Richards. J. C. (eds) 2009. *The Cambridge Guide to Second Language Teacher Education*. New York: Cambridge University Press.

Caruso, J. J. 1977. Phases in Student Teaching. *Young Children*, 33, 57–63.

Clair, N. 1998. Teacher Study Groups: Persistent Questions in a Promising Approach. *TESOL Quarterly*, 32, 465–492.

Clarke, A. 1995. Professional Development in Practicum Settings: Reflective Practice Under Scrutiny. *Teaching and Teacher Education*, 11, 243–261.

Cohen, J. 2008. "That's Not Treating You as a Professional": Teachers Constructing Complex Professional Identities through Talk. *Teachers and Teaching*, 14, 2, 79–93

Cooper,C Boyd. J. (1998). Creating Sustained Professional Growth Through Collaborative Reflection. In C. M. Brody and N. Davidson (eds), *Professional Development for Cooperative Learning: Issues and Approaches*. New York: State University of New York Press, 26–49.

Cormany, S., Maynor, C., and Kalnin, J. 2005. Developing Self, Developing Curriculum and Developing Theory: Researchers in Residence at Patrick Henry Professional Practice School. In D. J. Tedick (ed.), *Second Language Education: International Perspective*. Mahwah; NJ: Lawrence Erlbaum Associates Publishers, 215–230.

Creswell, J. 1994. *Research Design: Qualitative and Quantitative Approaches.* Thousand Oaks, CA: Sage

Crow, J. and Smith, L. 2005. Co-Teaching in Higher Education: Reflective Conversation on Shared Experience as Continued Professional Development for Lecturers and Health and Social Care Students. *Reflective Practice,* 6(4), 491–506.

Dewey, 1916. *Democracy and Education.* New York: Macmillan.

Dewey, J. 1933. *How We Think: A Restatement of the Relation of Reflective Thinking to the Educative Process.* Boston: Houghton-Mifflin.

Downey, C., Steffy, B., English, F., Frase, L., and Poston, W. 2004. *The Three-Minute Classroom Walk-Through.* Thousand Oaks: Corwin Press.

Duff, P. and Uchida, Y. 1997. The Negotiation of Teachers' Sociocultural Identities and Practices in Postsecondary EFL Classrooms. *TESOL Quarterly,* 31, 451–486

Ericsson, K.A. and Smith, J. (eds) 1991. *Toward a General Theory of Expertise.* Cambridge: Cambridge University Press.

Farrell, T.S.C. 2007. *Reflective Language Teaching: from Research to Practice.* London: Continuum Press.

Farrell, T.S.C. 2013. *Reflective Writing for Language Teachers.* London, UK: Equinox.

Fessler, R. and Christensen, J. C. 1992. *The Teacher Career Cycle: Understanding and Guiding the Professional Development of Teachers.* Boston: Allyn and Bacon.

Freeman, D. 1982. Observing Teachers: Three Approaches to in–Service Training and Development. *TESOL Quarterly,* 16, 21–28.

Freeman, D. 1992. Language Teacher Education, Emerging discourse, and change in classroom practice. In J. Flowerdew, M. Brock, & S. Hsia (eds), *Perspectives on language teacher education.* Hong Kong: City Polytechnic of Hong Kong, 1–21.

Freeman, D. 1996. Redefining the Relationship between Research and What Teachers Know. In K. M., Bailey and Nunan, D., (eds), *Voices from the Language Classroom: Qualitative Research in Second Language Education.* Cambridge: Cambridge University Press, 88–115.

Fuller, F.F. and Brown, O. H. 1975. Becoming a Teacher. In K. Ryan (ed.), *Teacher Education* (74th Yearbook of the national society for the study of education. Part II). Chicago: University of Chicago Press, 25–52.

Garton, S. and Richards, K (eds) 2008. *Professional Encounters in TESOL: Discourses of Teachers in Teaching.* Basingstoke: Palgrave Macmillan.

Glesne, C. and Peshkin, A. 1992. *Becoming Qualitative Researchers: An Introduction.* New York: Longman.

Goodson, I. 1994. Studying Teachers' Life and Work. *Teaching and Teacher Education,* 10, 29–37.

Hargraves, A. 1996. "Revisiting Voice". *Educational Researcher,* 25/1: 12–19.

Hatton, N. and Smith, D. 1995. Reflection in Teacher Education: Towards Definition and Implementation. *Teaching and Teacher Education,* 11, 33–49.

Hawkins, M. and Norton, B 2009. Critical Language Teacher Education. In A. Burns and J. Richards (eds), *Cambridge Guide to Second Language Teacher Education.* Cambridge: Cambridge University Press, 30–39.

Huberman, M.A. 1989. The Professional Life Cycle of Teachers. *Teachers College Record,* 9, 1, 31–57.

Huberman, M.A. 1993. *The Lives of Teachers.* New York: Teachers College Press.

Huberman, M. 1995. Professional Careers and Professional Development: Some Intersections. In T. Guskey and M. Huberman (eds), *Professional Development in Education: New Paradigms & Practices.* New York: Teachers College Press, 193–224.

Humaira, A. and Rarieya, J.F.A., 2008. Teacher Development through Reflective Conversations – Possibilities and Tensions: A Pakistan Case. *Reflective Practice*, 9, 269–279.

Jackson, P. W. 1968. *Life in Classrooms.* New York: Holt, Rhinehart, Winston.

Jalongo, M. R. and Isenberg, J. P. 1995. *Teachers' Stories: From Personal Narrative to Professional Insight.* San Francisco: Jossey-Bass.

Jay, J. K. and Johnson, K. L. 2002. Capturing Complexity: A Typology of Reflective Practice for Teacher Education. *Teaching and Teacher Education*, 18, 73–85.

Johnson, K. E. and Golombek, P. R. (eds). 2002. *Narrative Inquiry as Professional Development.* New York: Cambridge University Press.

Johnson, K. 2003. *Designing Language Teaching Tasks.* Basingstoke, UK: Palgrave Macmillan.

Johnson, K. (ed) 2005. *Expertise in Second Language Learning and Teaching.* Basingstoke, UK: Palgrave Macmillan.

Jorgensen, D. 1989. *Participant Observation: A Methodology for Human Studies.* Newbury Park, CA: Sage Publications.

Katz, L. G. 1972. Developmental Stages of Preschool Teachers. *Elementary School Journal*, 73, 50–54.

Kiely, R. and Davis, M. 2010. From Transmission to Transformation: Teacher Learning in English for Speakers of Other Languages. *Language Teaching Research*, 14, 3, 277–295.

Kreisberg, S. 1992. Transforming power: Domination, Empowerment, and Education. Albany, NY: State University of New York Press.

Kumaravadivelu, B. 2012. *Language Teacher Education for a Global Society.* New York: Routledge.

Lange, D. 1990. A Blueprint for a Teacher Development Program. In J. C. Richards and D. Nunan (eds), *Second Language Teacher Education.* New York: Cambridge University Press, 245–268.

Leung, C. 2009. Second Language Teacher Professionalism. In A. Burns and J. C. Richards (eds), *The Cambridge Guide to Second Language Teacher Education.* Cambridge, UK: Cambridge University Press, 49–58.

Lincoln, Y. S. and Guba, E. G. 1985. *Naturalistic Inquiry.* Beverly Hills: Sage.

Lortie, D. C. 1975. *Schoolteacher: A Sociological Study.* Chicago: University of Chicago Press.

McCabe, A. 2002. A Wellspring for Development. In J. Edge (ed.) *Continuing Professional Development.* Whitstable, UK: IATEFL Publications, 82–96.

McDonald, F. J. 1982. *A Theory of the Professional Development of Teachers.* Paper presented at the meeting of the American Educational Research Association, New York.

Mann, S. 2005. The Language Teacher's Development. *Language Teaching*, 38, 103–118.

Meister, D.G and Ahrens, P. 2011. Resisting Plateauing: Four Veteran Teachers' Stories. *Teaching and Teacher Education*, 27, 4, 770–778.

Merriam, S. B. 1988. *Case Study Research in Education: A Qualitative Approach.* San Francisco: Jossey–Bass.

Merriam, S. B. 2001. *Qualitative Research and Case Study Applications in Education.* San Francisco: Jossey-Bass.

Miles, M. B. and Huberman, A. M. 1984. *Qualitative Data Analysis: A Source Book of New Methods*. Newbury Park, CA: Sage Publications.

Milstein, M. M. 1989. Plateauing as an occupational phenomenon among teachers and administrators. Paper presented at the annual meeting of the American Educational Research Association, San Francisco, CA (ERIC Document Reproduction Service No. ED 306 675).

Oberg, A. and Blades, C. 1990. The Spoken and the Unspoken: The Story of an Educator. *Phenomonology+Pedagogy*, 8, 161–180.

Oprandy, R. Golden, L, and Shiomi, K. 1999. Teachers Talking about Teaching. In J. Gebhard and R. Oprandy (eds), *Language Teaching Awareness*. New York: Cambridge University Press, 149–171.

Richards, J.C. and Farrell, T.S.C 2005. *Professional Development for Language Teachers*. New York: Cambridge University Press.

Richards, J. C and Lockhard, C. 1994. *Reflective Teaching*. New York: Cambridge University Press.

Richards, J.C. (ed). 1998. *Beyond Training: Perspectives on Language Teacher Education*. New York: Cambridge University Press

Richards, J. C., Li, B. and Tang, A. 1998. Exploring Pedagogical Reasoning Skills. In J. C. Richards (ed.), *Beyond Training: Perspectives on Language Teacher Education*. New York: Cambridge University Press, 86–102.

Richardson., L., 1997. *Fields of Play: Constructing an Academic Life*. New Brunswick, NJ: Rutgers University Press.

Rodríguez, A. and McKay, S. 2010. *Professional Development for Experienced Teachers Working With Adult English Language Learners*. CAEL Brief: Center for Applied Linguistics, Washington, D.C. USA.

Rosenholtz, S. J. and Simpson, C. 1990. Workplace conditions and the rise and fall of teachers' commitment. *Sociology of Education*, 63, 4, 241–257.

Saracho, O.N. 2000. A Framework for Effective Classroom Teaching. In R. J. Riding and S. G. Rayner (eds), *International Perspectives on Individual Differences. Volume 1: Cognitive Styles*. Stamford, CT: Ablex Publishing, 297–314.

Schön, D. A. 1983. *The Reflective Practitioner: How Professionals Think in Action*. New York: Basic Books.

Schön, D. A. 1987. *Educating the Reflective Practitioner: Towards a New Design for Teaching and Learning in the Profession*. San Francisco: Jossey-Bass.

Sprinthall, N. A. and Theis-Sprinthall, L. 1980. Educating for Teacher Growth: A Cognitive Developmental Perspective. *Theory Into Practice*, 19, 278–286.

Thiel, T. 1999. Reflections on Critical Incidents. *Prospect*, 14, 44–52.

Tripp, D. 1993. *Critical Incidents in Teaching*. London: Rutledge.

Tsui, A. 2003. *Understanding Expertise in Teaching: Case Studies of ESL Teachers*. New York: Cambridge University Press

Tsui, A.B. 2005. Expertise in Teaching: Perspectives and Issues. In K. Johnson (ed.), *Expertise in Second Language Learning and Teaching*. NewYork: Palgrave Macmillan, 167–189.

Tsui, A.B. 2009. Teaching expertise: Approaches, perspectives, and characterization. In A. Burns and J. Richards (eds), *Cambridge Guide to Second Language Teacher Education*. Cambridge: Cambridge University Press, 190–197.

Urrieta, L. 2007. Figured Worlds and Education: An Introduction to the Special Issue. *The Urban Review*, 39, 2, 107–116.

Valli, L. 1997. Listening to Other Voices: A Description of Teacher Reflection in the United States. *Peabody Journal of Education*, 72, 1, 67–88.

Varghese, M., Morgan, B., Johnston, B., and Johnson, K. 2005. Theorizing Language Teacher Identity: Three Perspectives and beyond. *Journal of Language, Identity, and Education*, 4, 1, 21–44.

Volkman, M. J. and Anderson, M. A. 1998. Creating Professional Identity: Dilemmas and Metaphors of a First-Year Chemistry Teacher. *Science Education*, 82, 293–310.

Walkington, J. 2005. Becoming a Teacher; Encouraging Development of Teacher Identity through Reflective Practice. *Asia-Pacific Journal of Teacher Education*, 33, 1, 53–64

Wallace, M, J. 1991. *Teacher Training: A Reflective Approach*. Cambridge: Cambridge University Press.

Williams, M. and Burden, R. 1997. *Psychology for Language Teachers: a Social Constructivist Approach*. Cambridge: Cambridge University Press.

Woods, D. 1996. *Teacher Cognition in Language Teaching*: Cambridge: Cambridge University Press.

Wright, T. 2010. Second Language Teacher Education: Review of Recent Research on Practice. *Language Teaching*, 43, 3, 259–296.

Zeichner, K. and Liston, O. 1996. *Reflective Teaching*. New Jersey: Lawrence Earlbaum.

# Index

CPSIA information can be obtained at www.ICGtesting.com
Printed in the USA
BVOW09*1849281214

380492BV00002B/11/P